Tattoo Flash

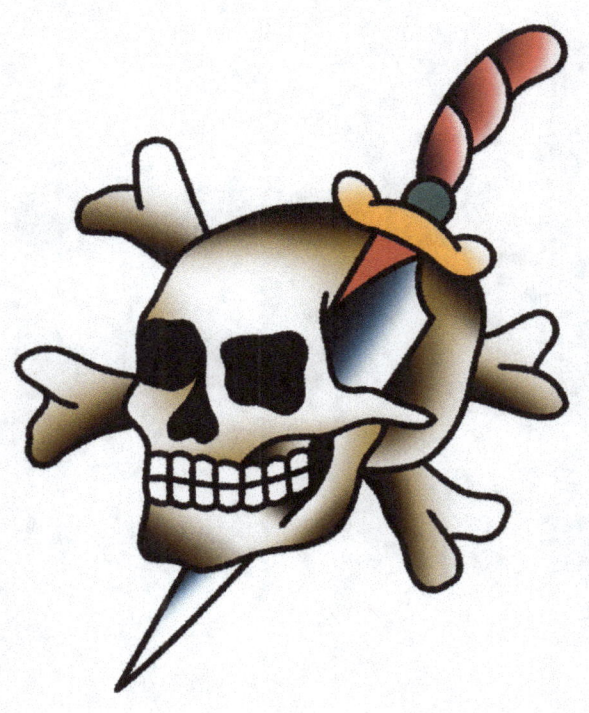

M.S. Hirsch

Copyright

Copyright@ 2026 by Hellbound Publishing

All rights reserved. No parts of this publication may be reproduced or utilized in any form or by any means, without prior permission from Publisher. You are permitted to use the illustrations in this book for creative designs or artwork. This book is for educational and artistic purposes only.

ISBN: 9789083662206

Preface

This book was born out of my passion for American Traditional Flash. Within this collection, you will find over 300 designs, carefully curated for everyone who shares a love for this iconic style.
I invite you to use these designs as a source of inspiration and reference material for your next tattoo. Whether you are a collector or an artist, I hope these pages spark your creativity. Thank you for sharing the passion for this timeless style.

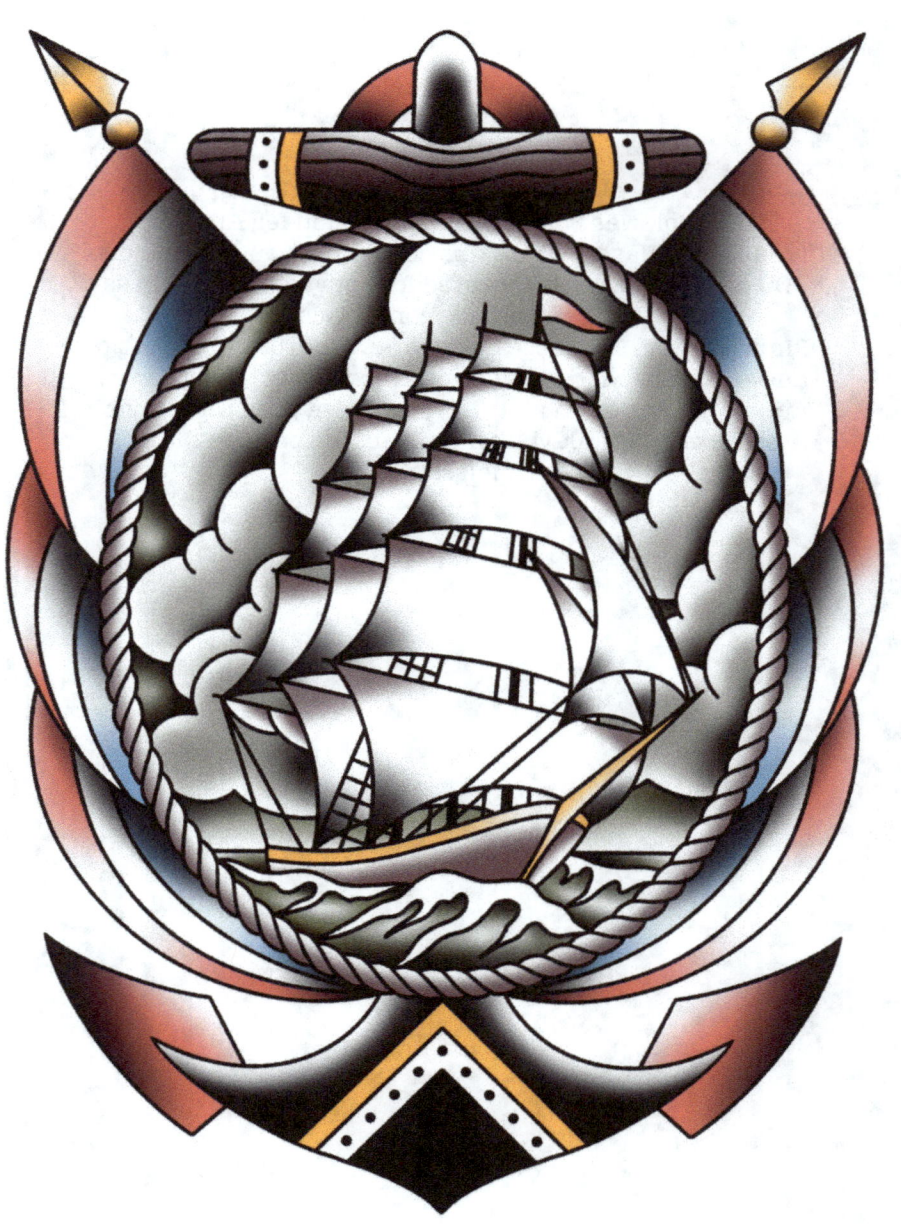

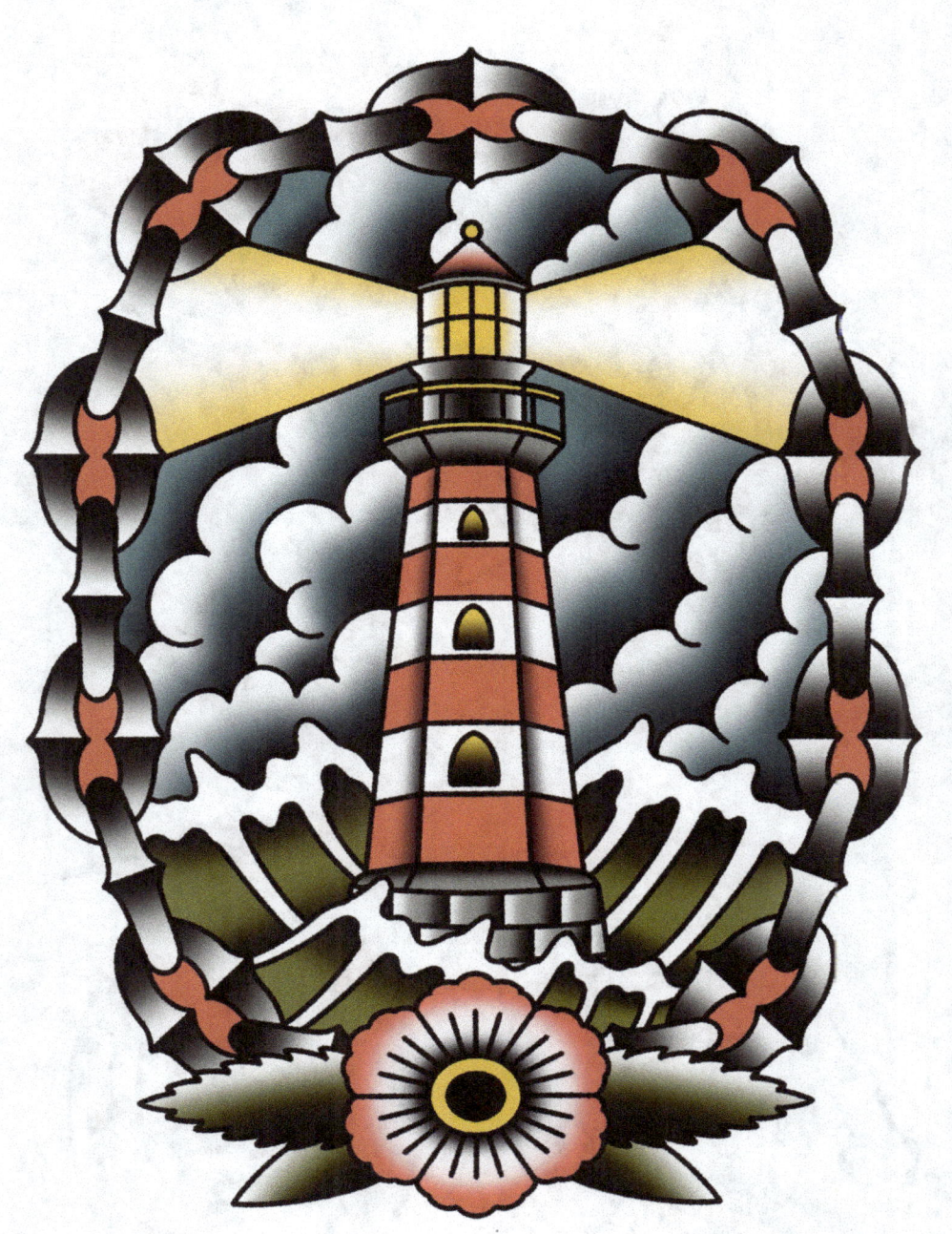

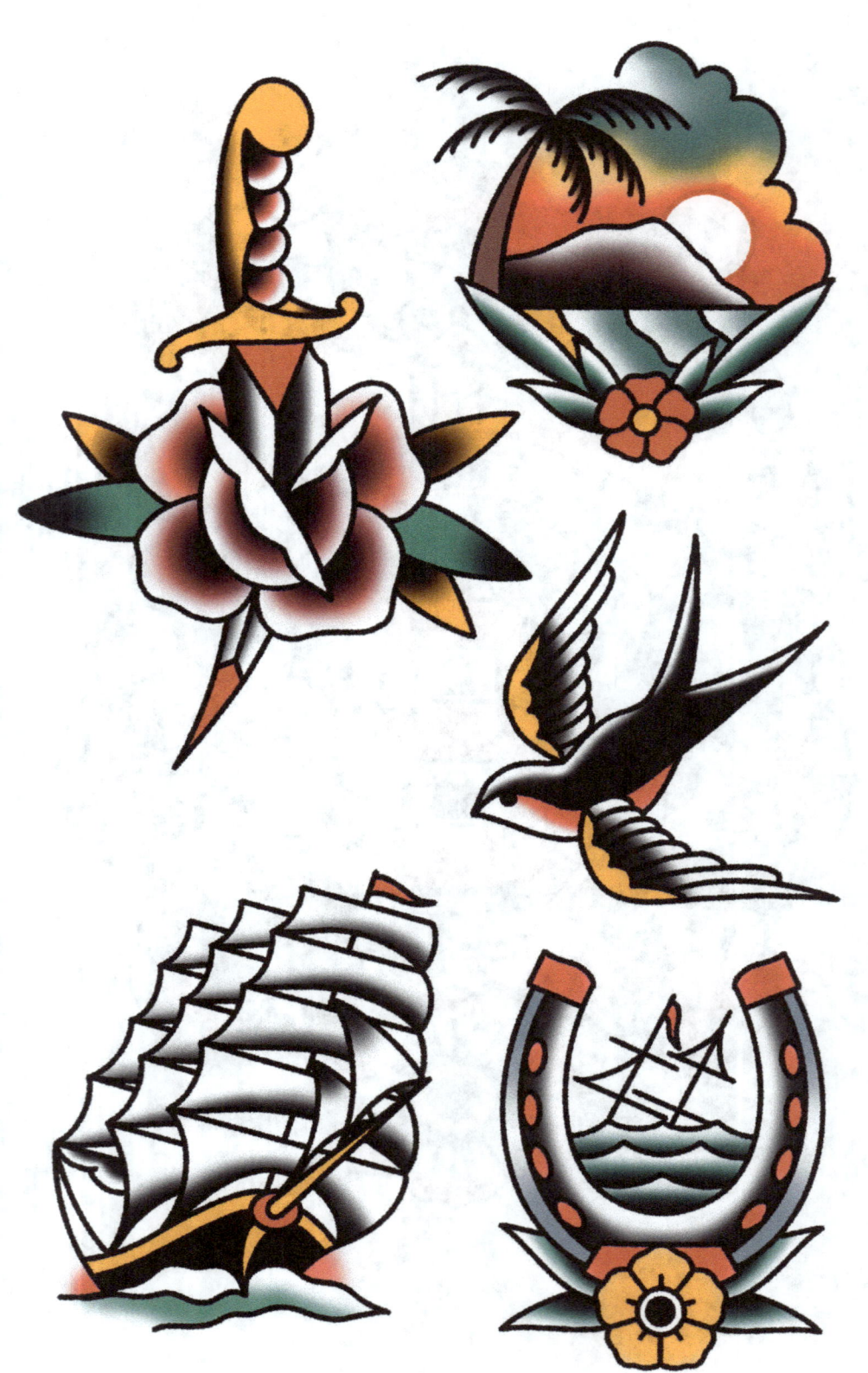

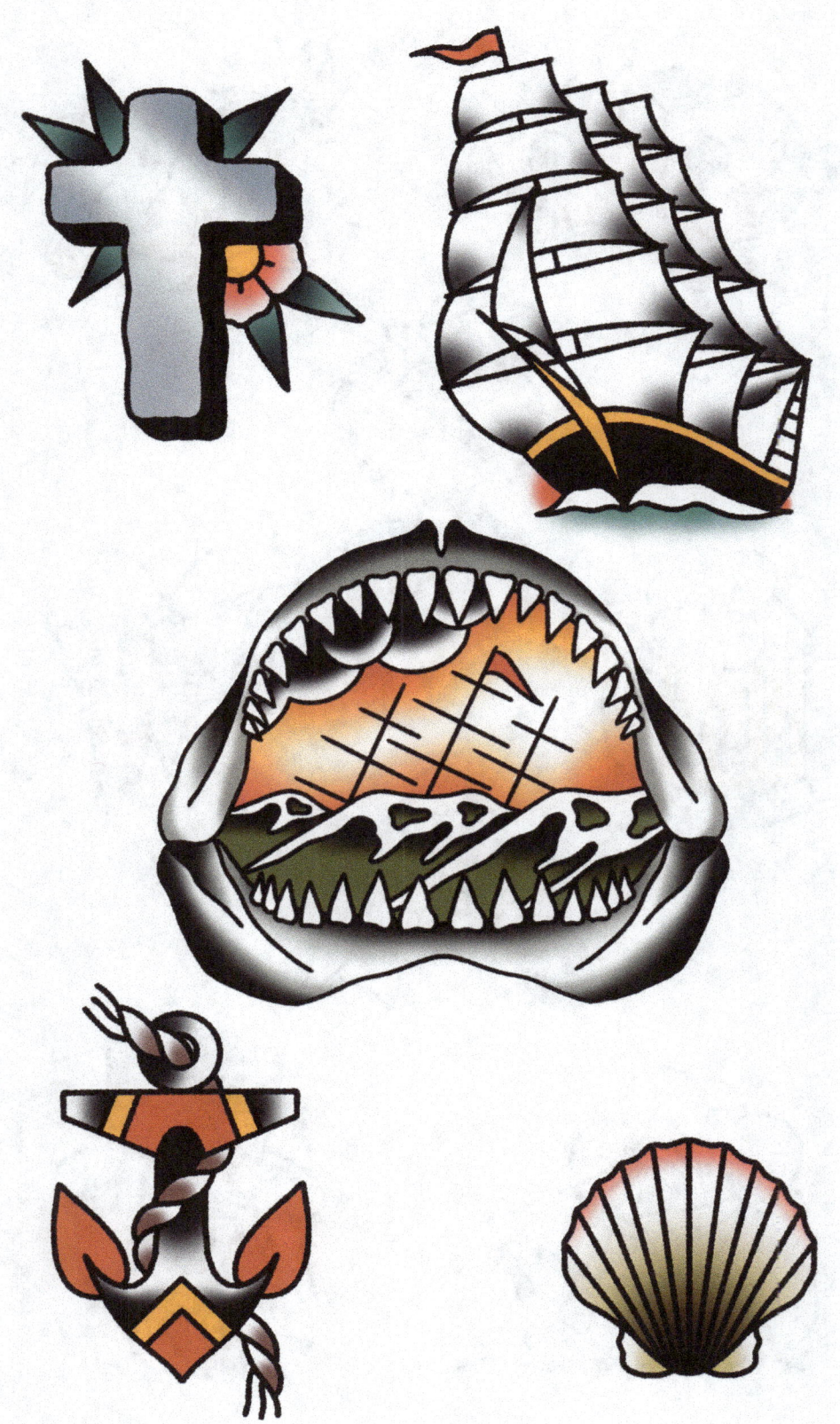

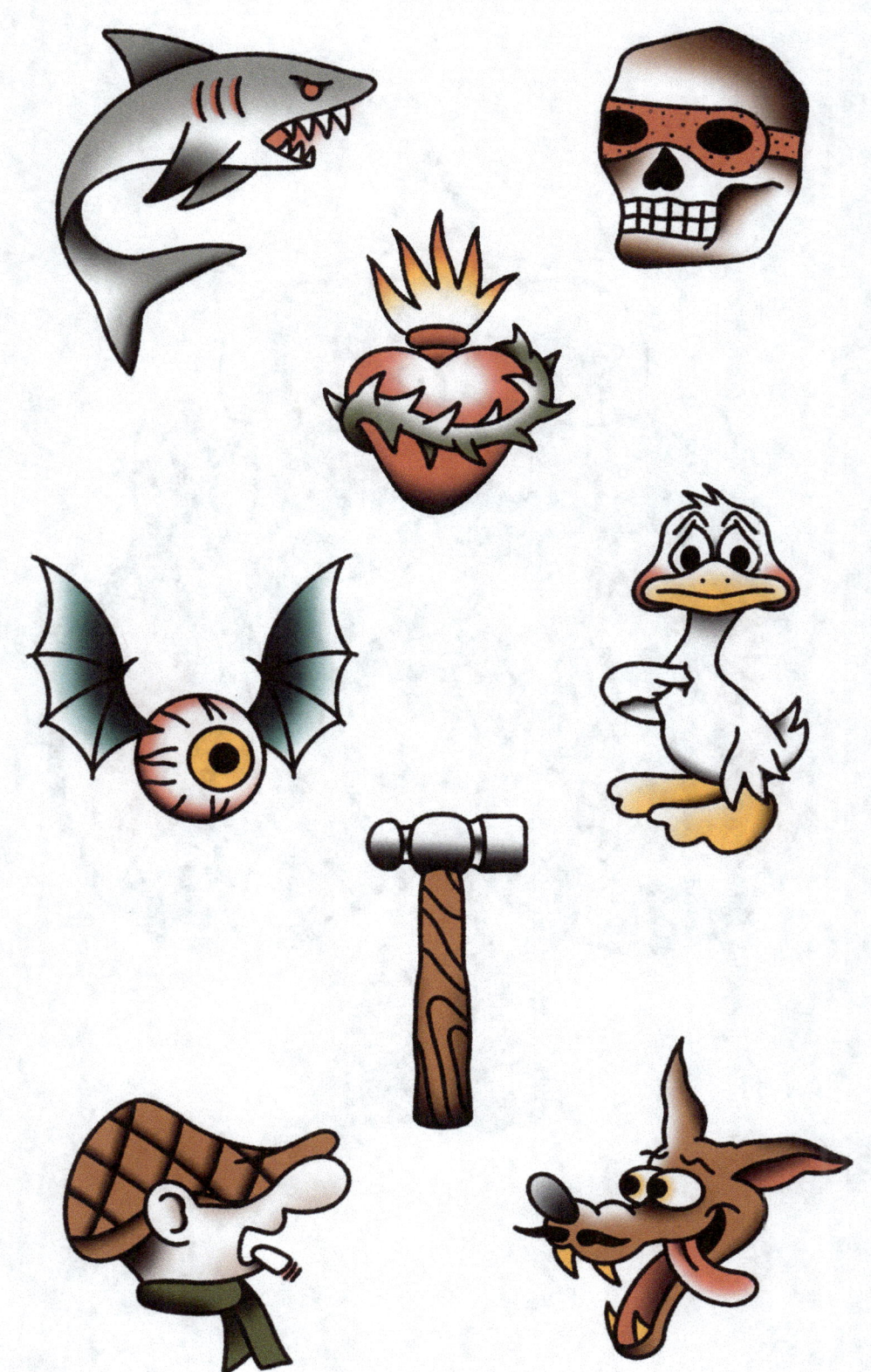

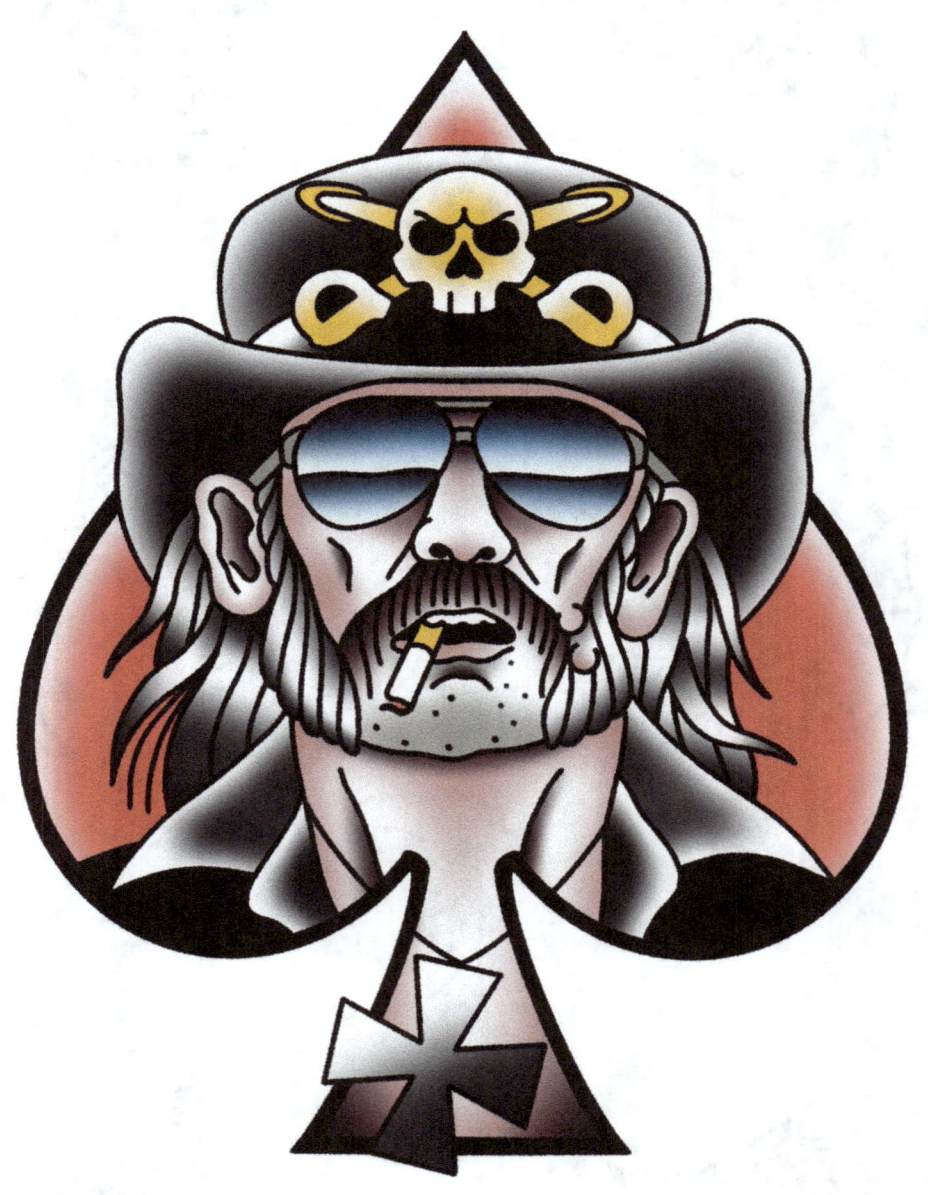

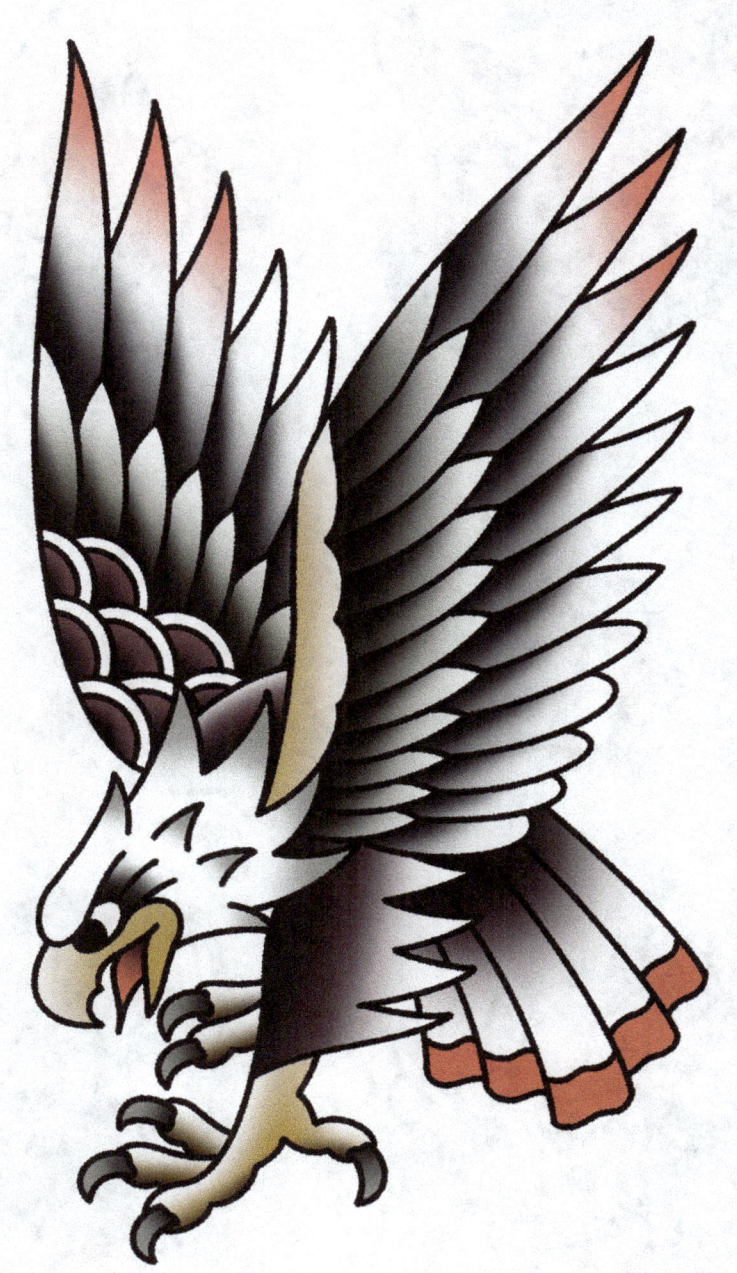

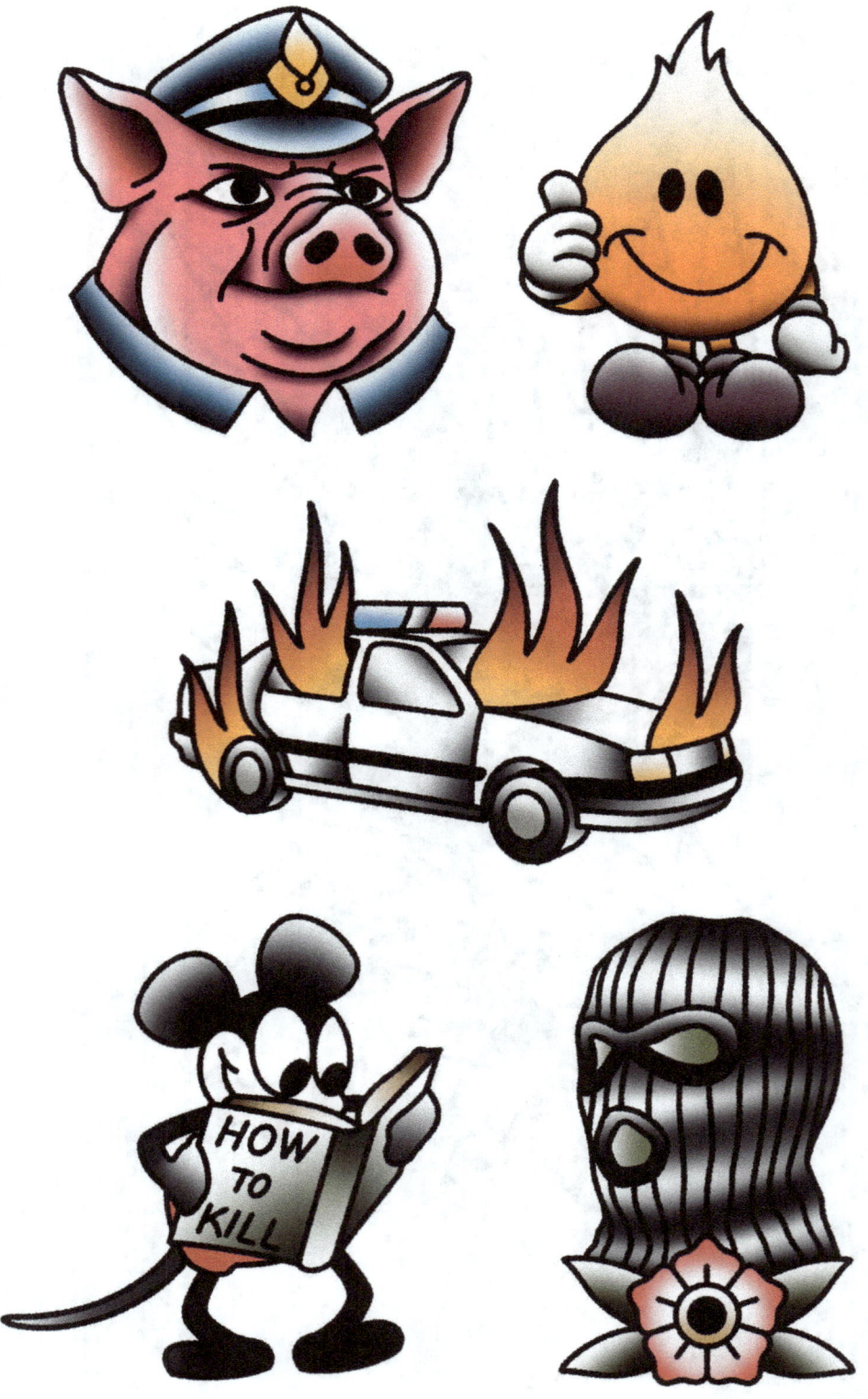

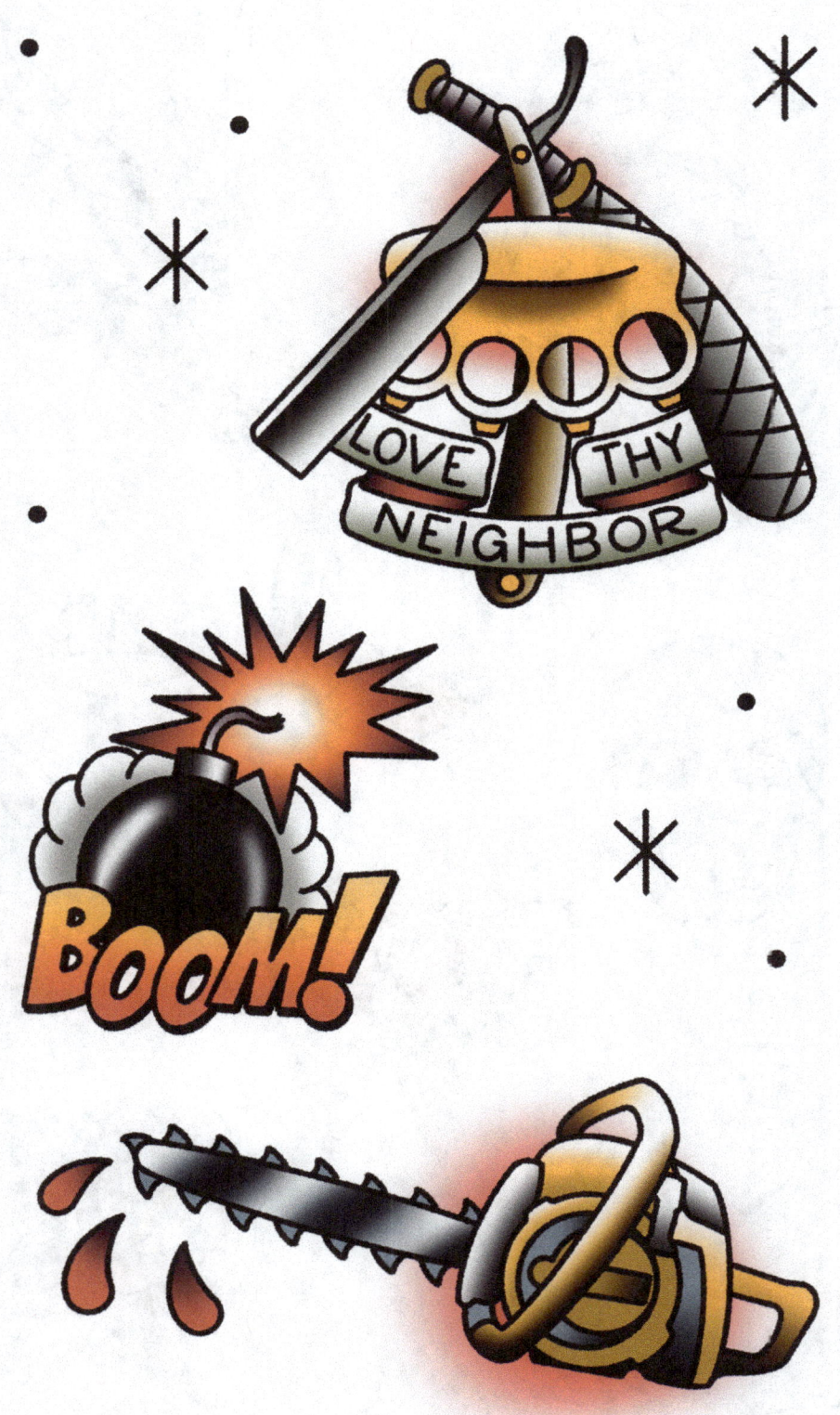

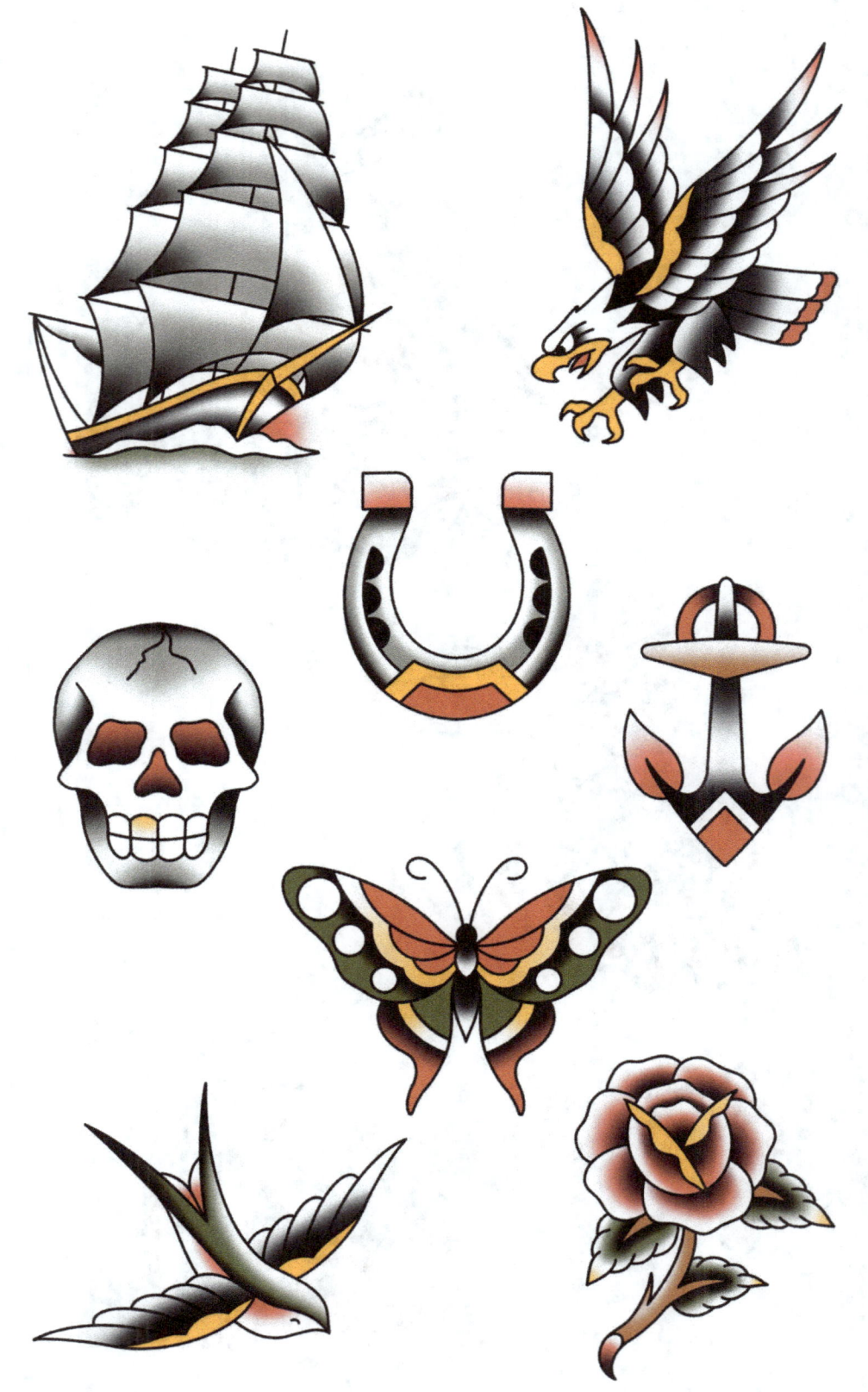

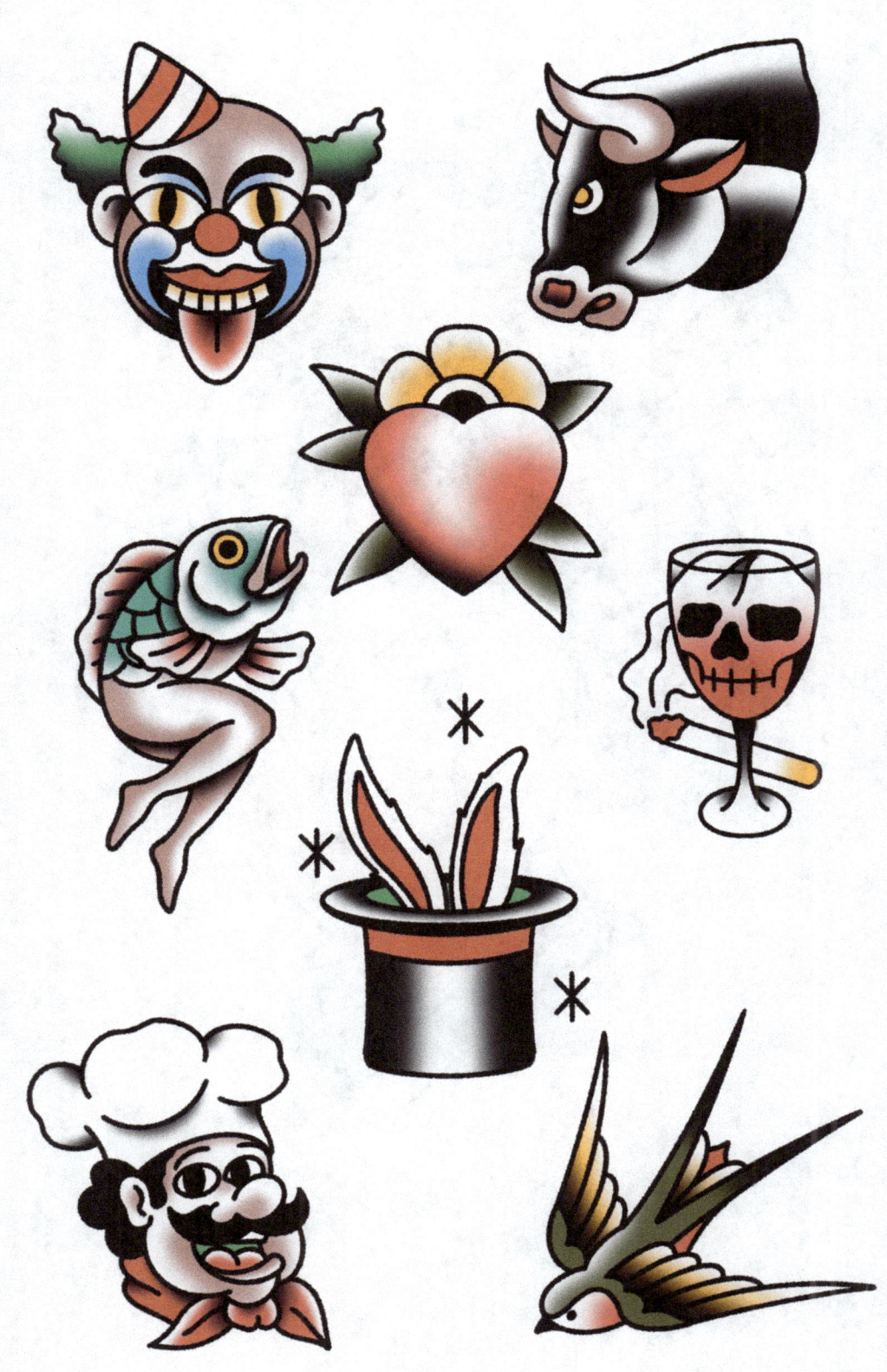

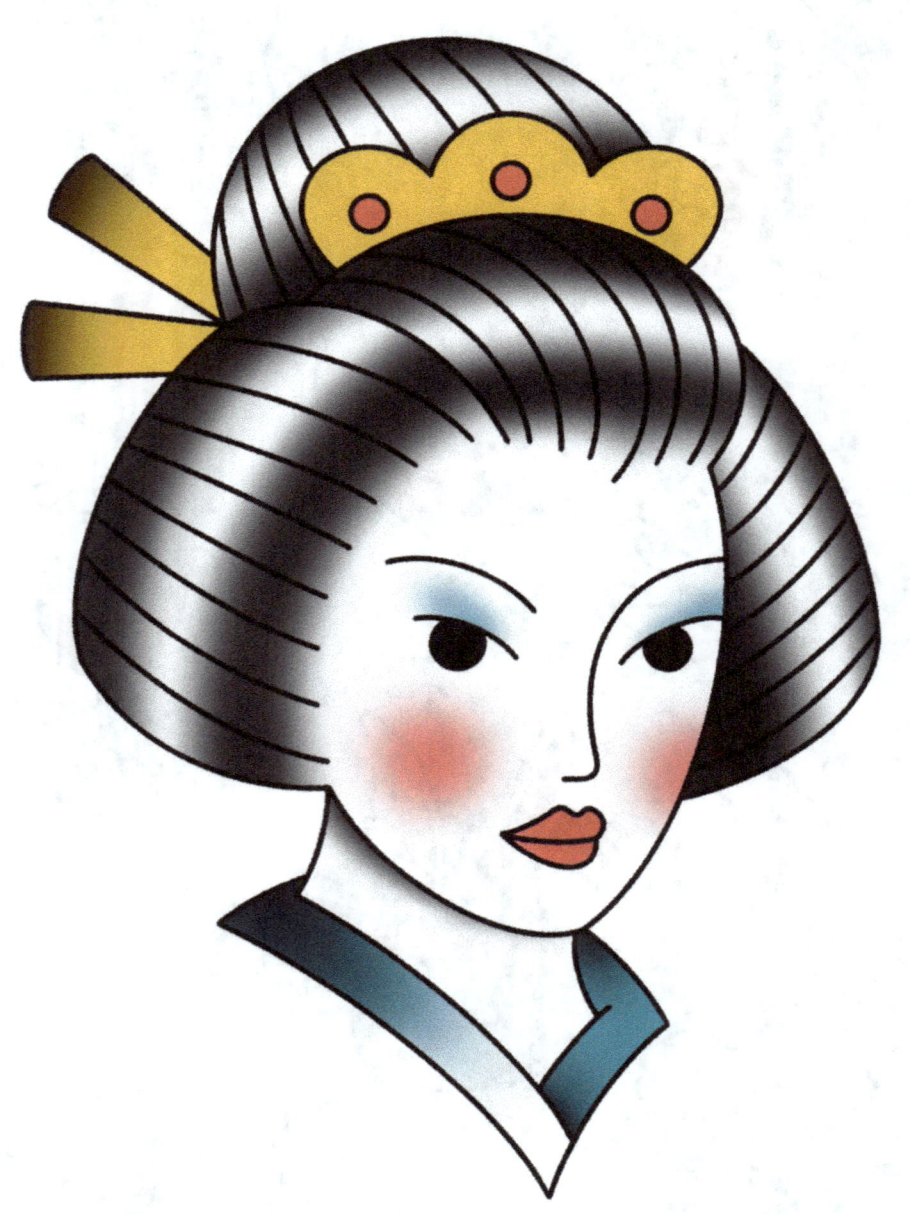

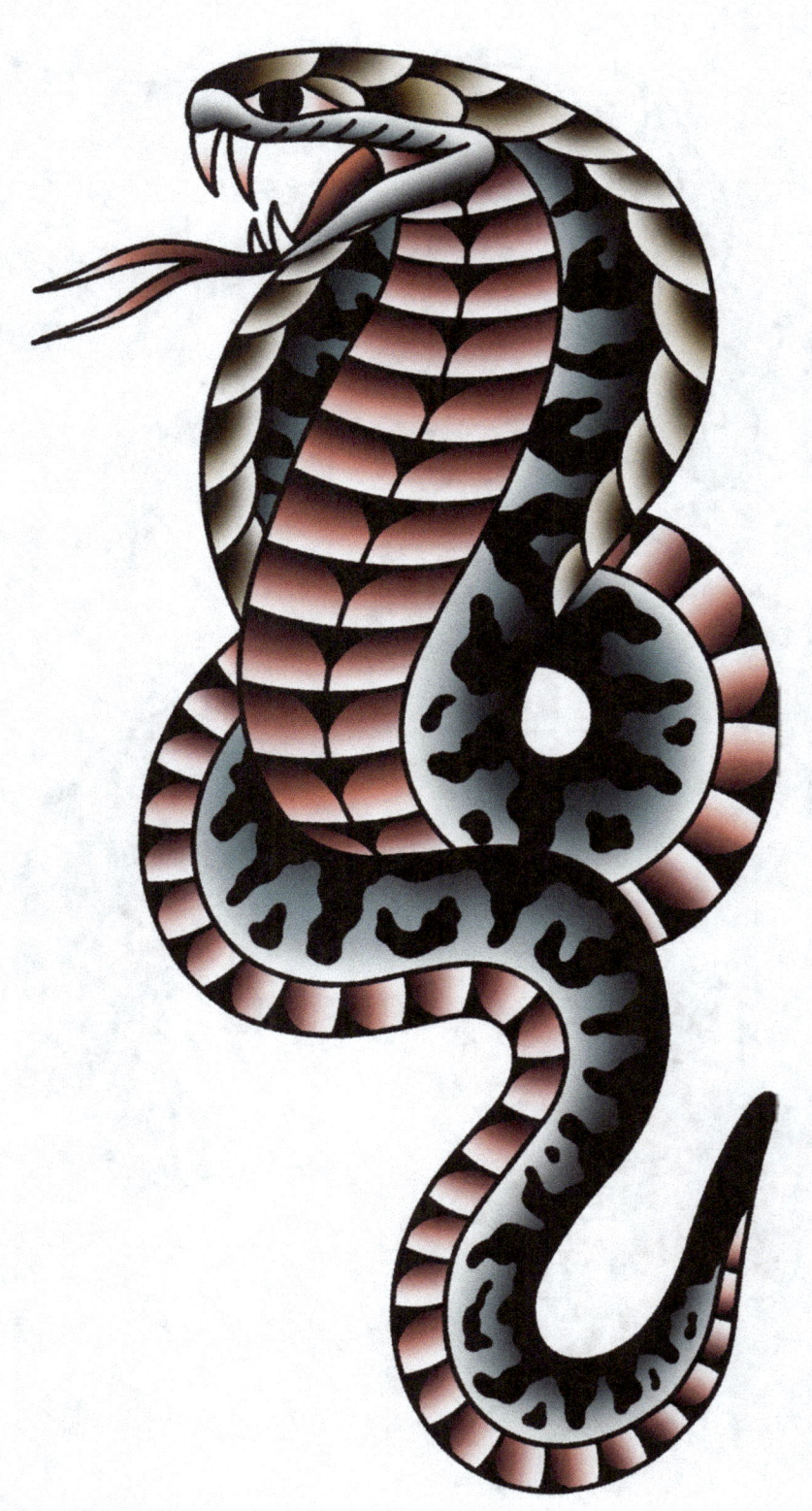

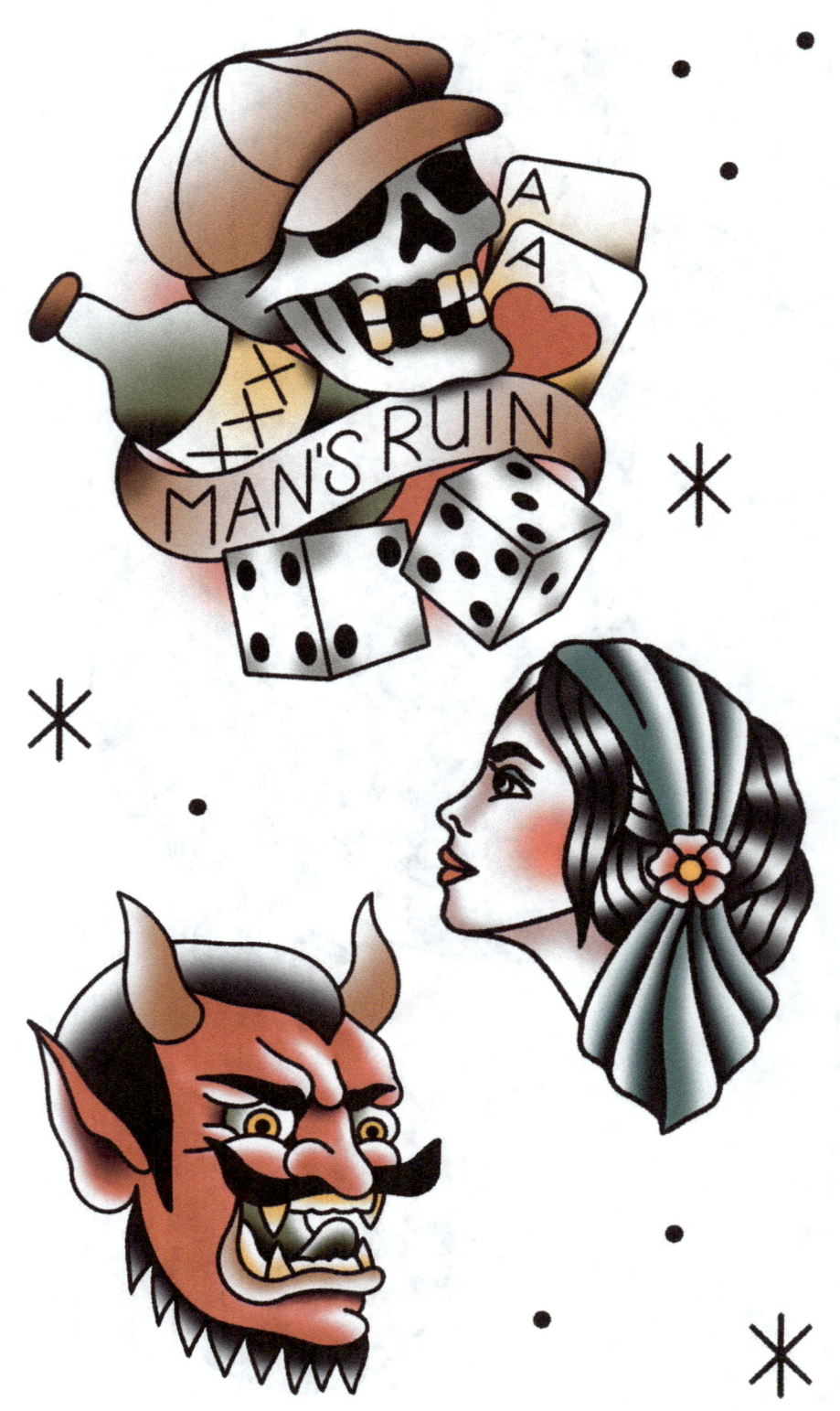

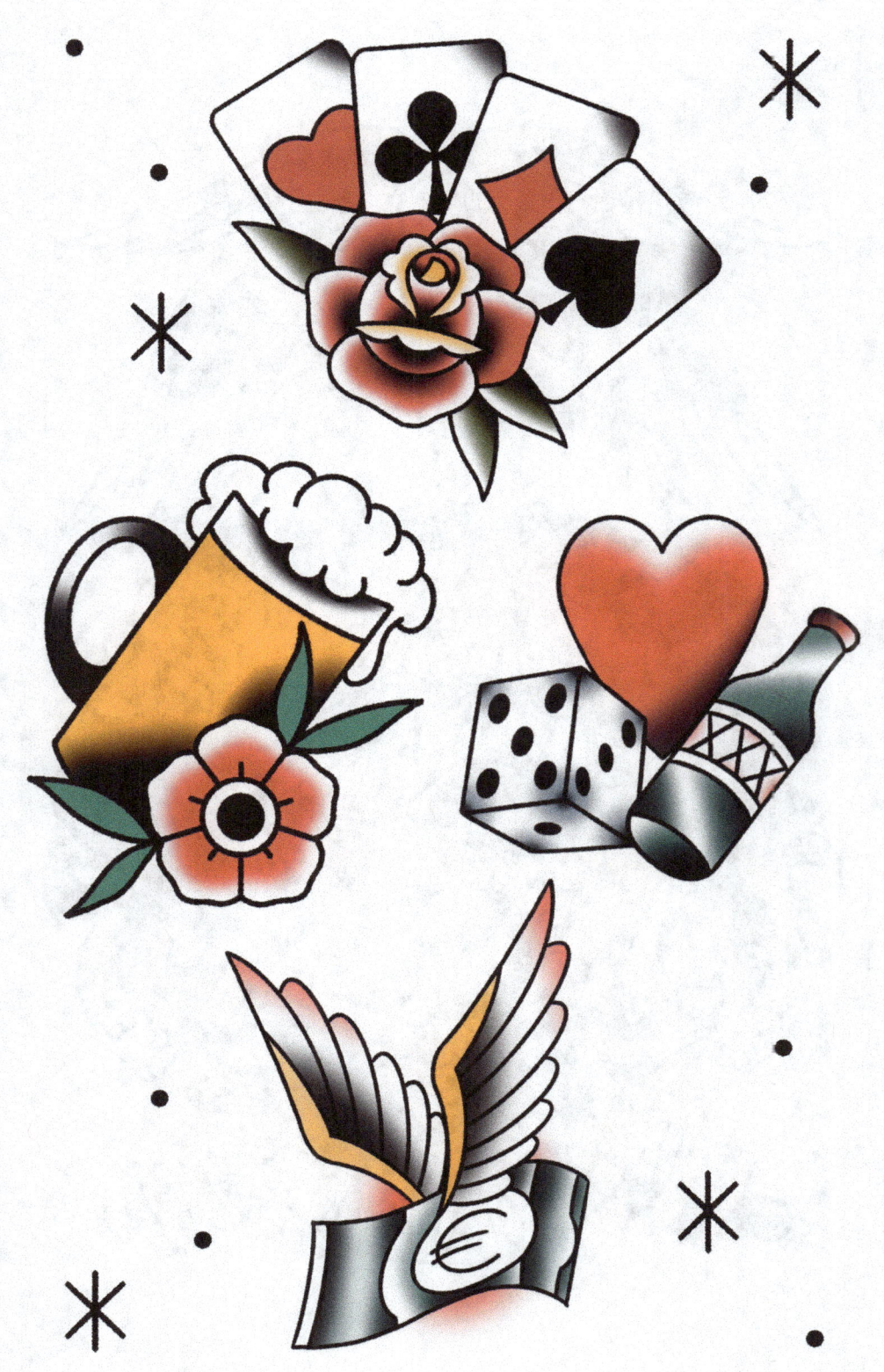

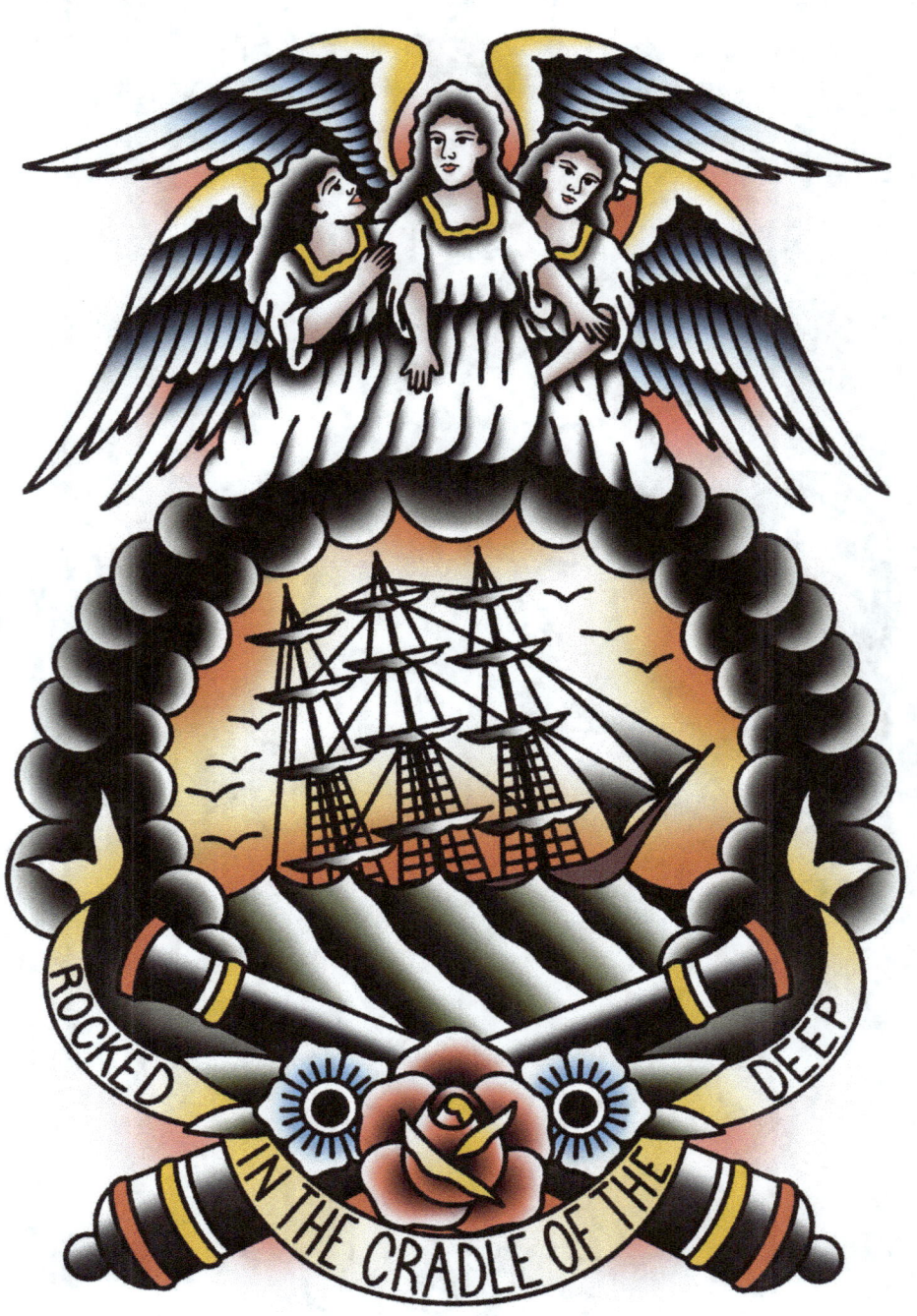

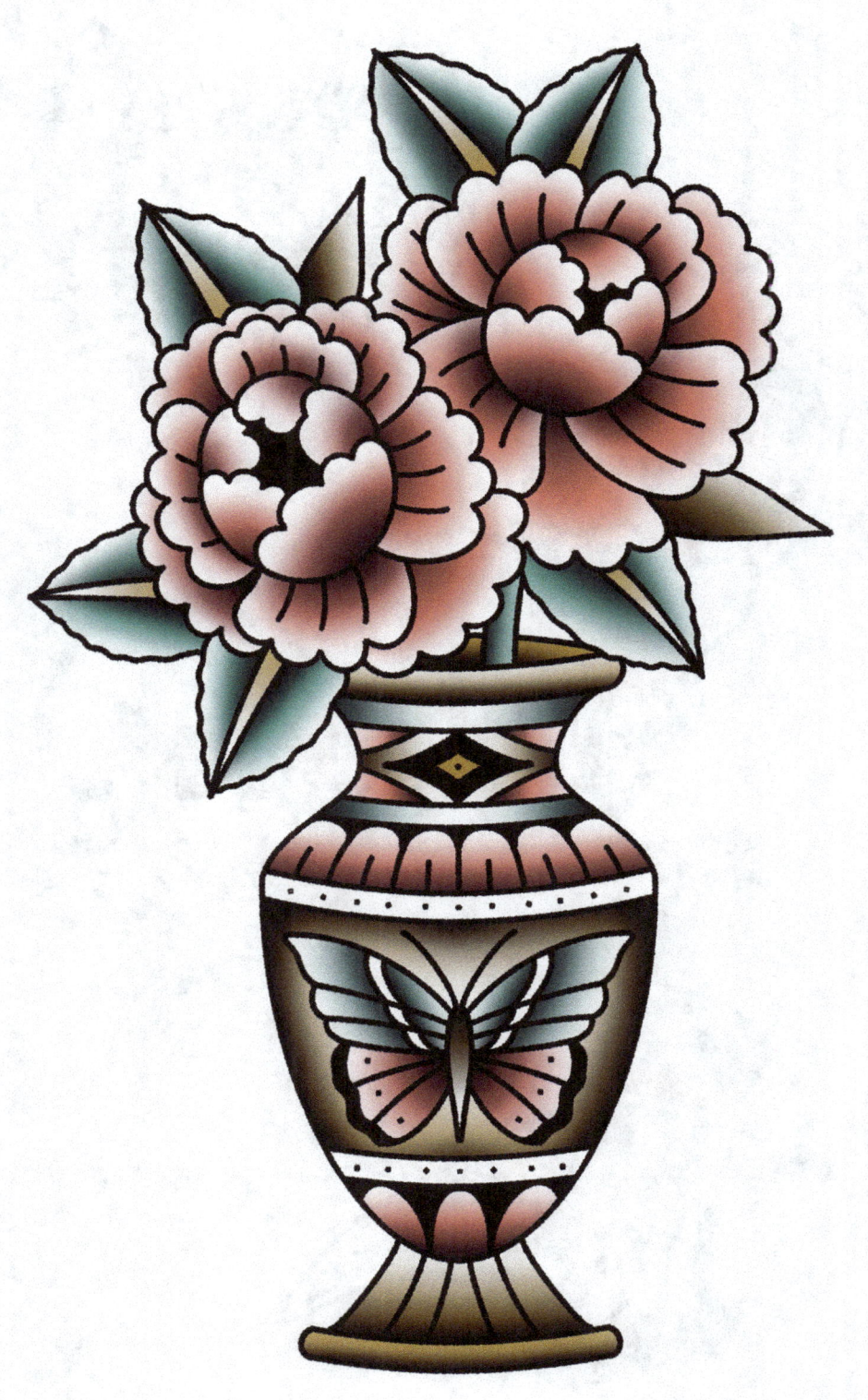

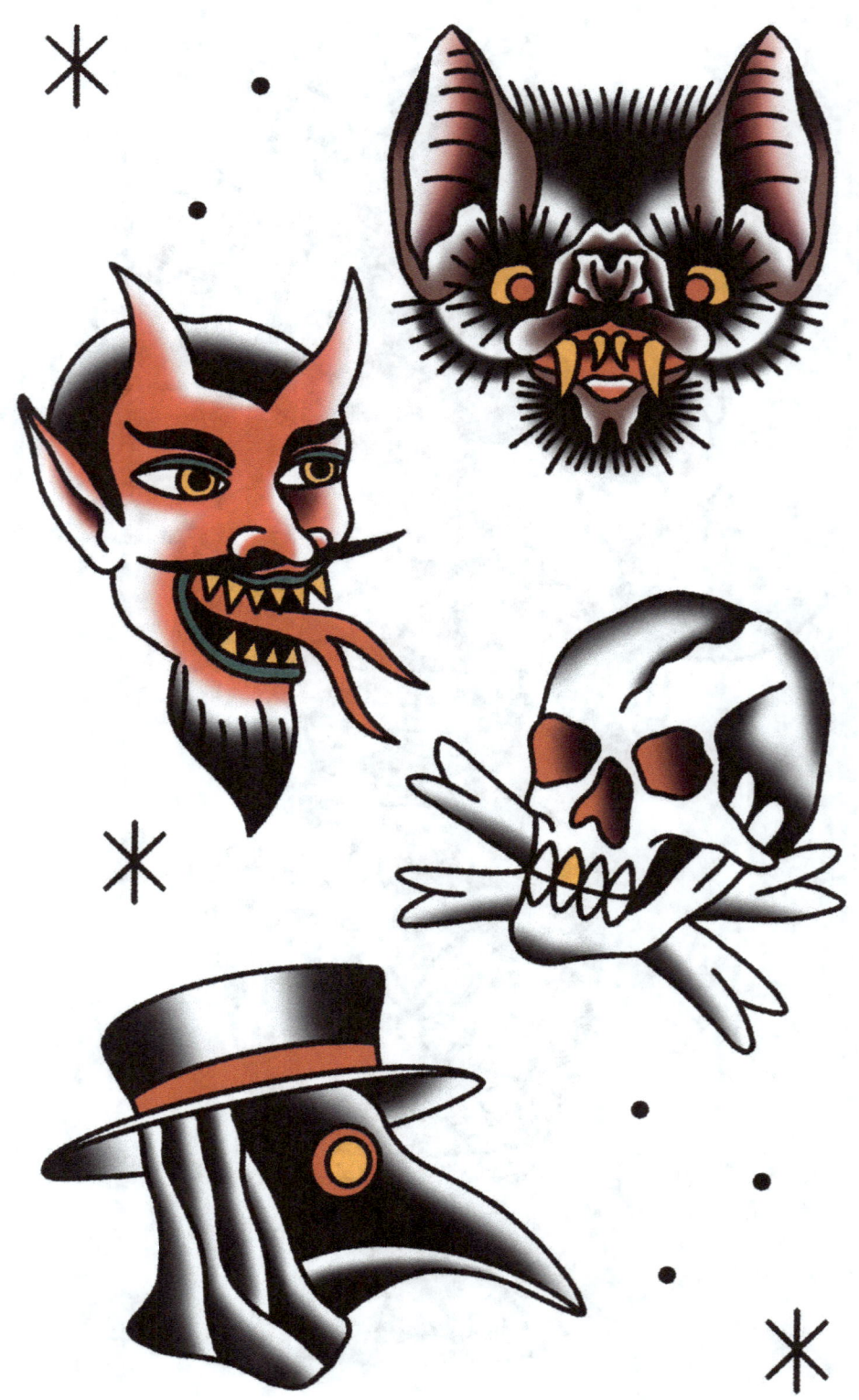

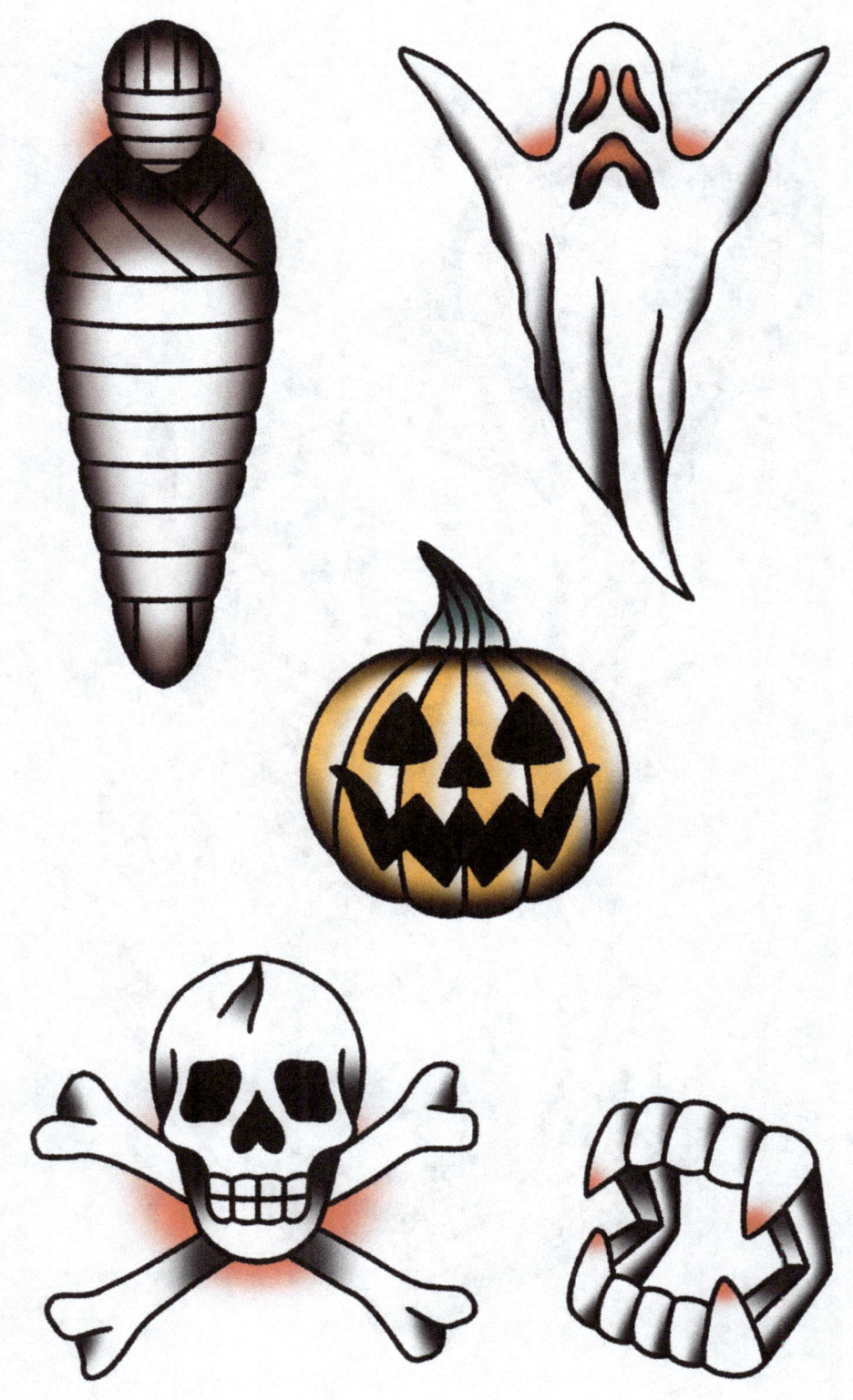

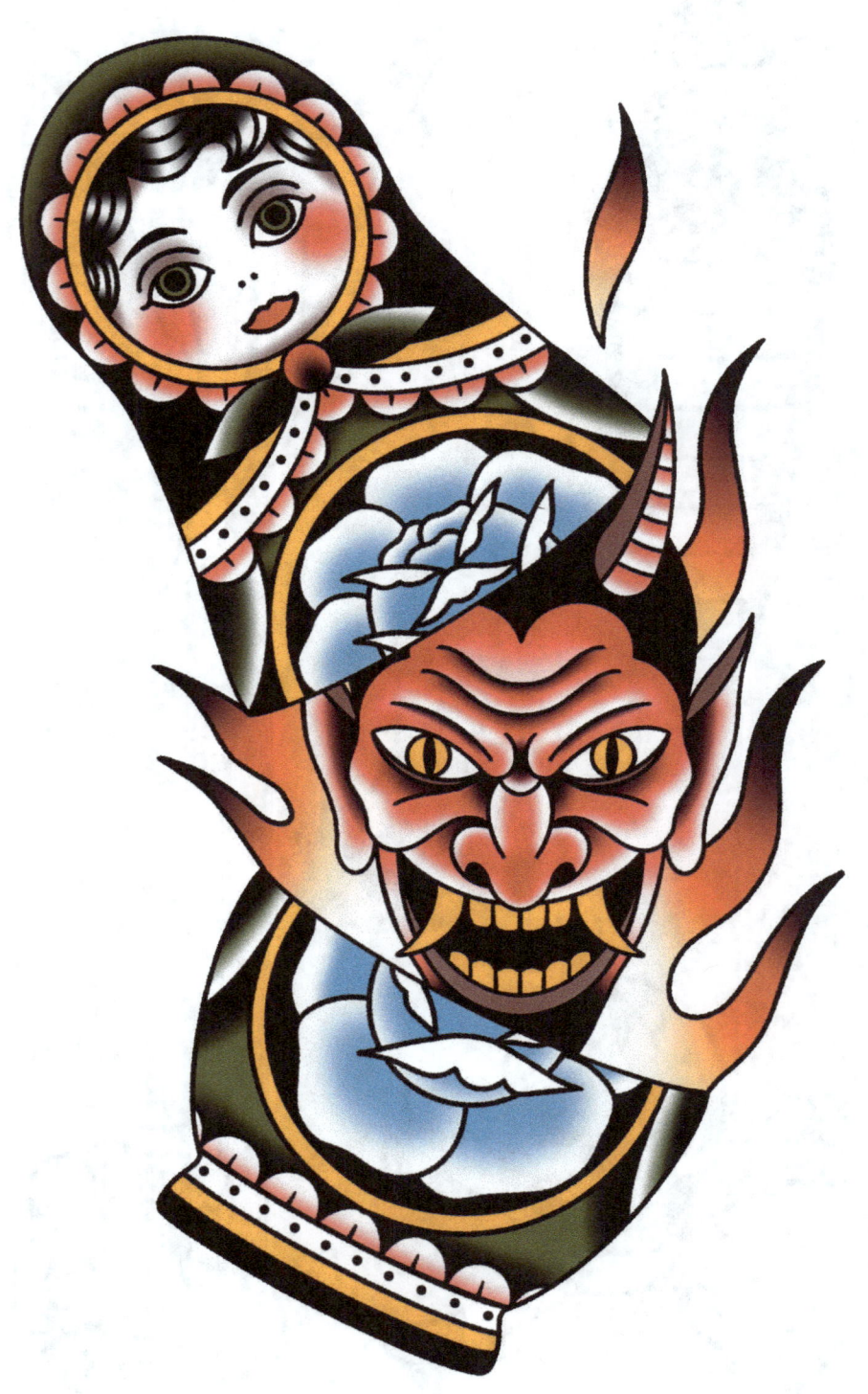

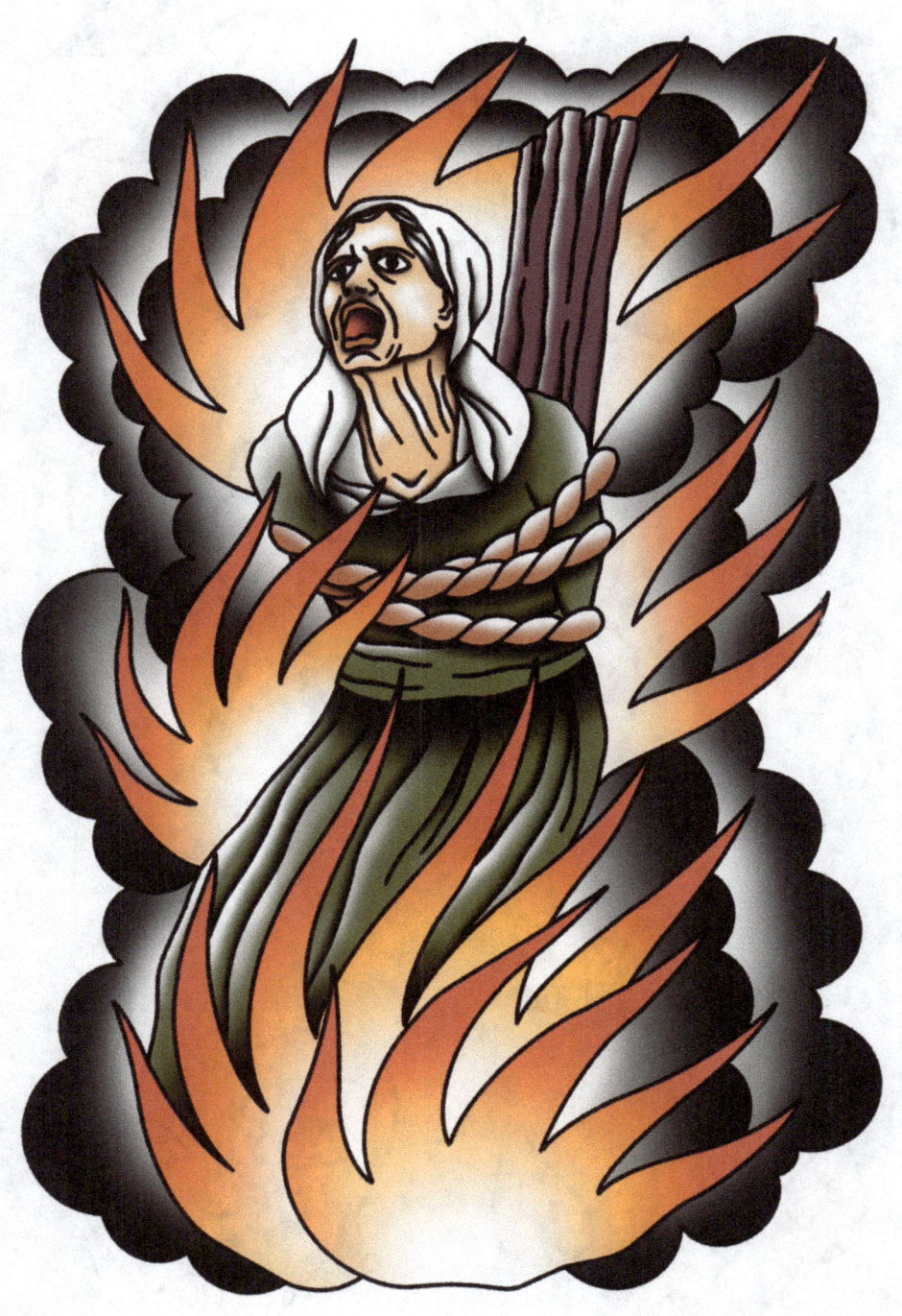

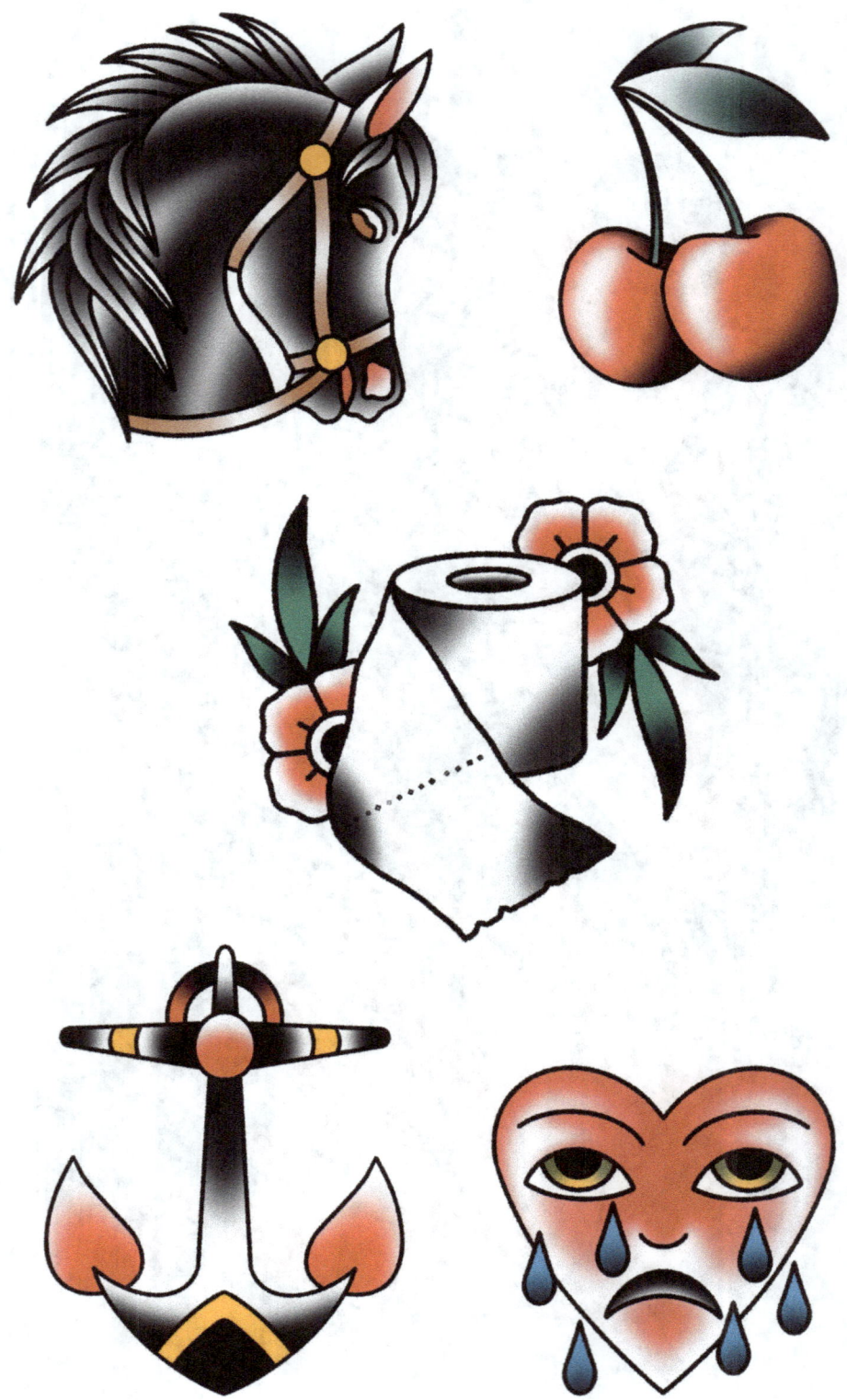

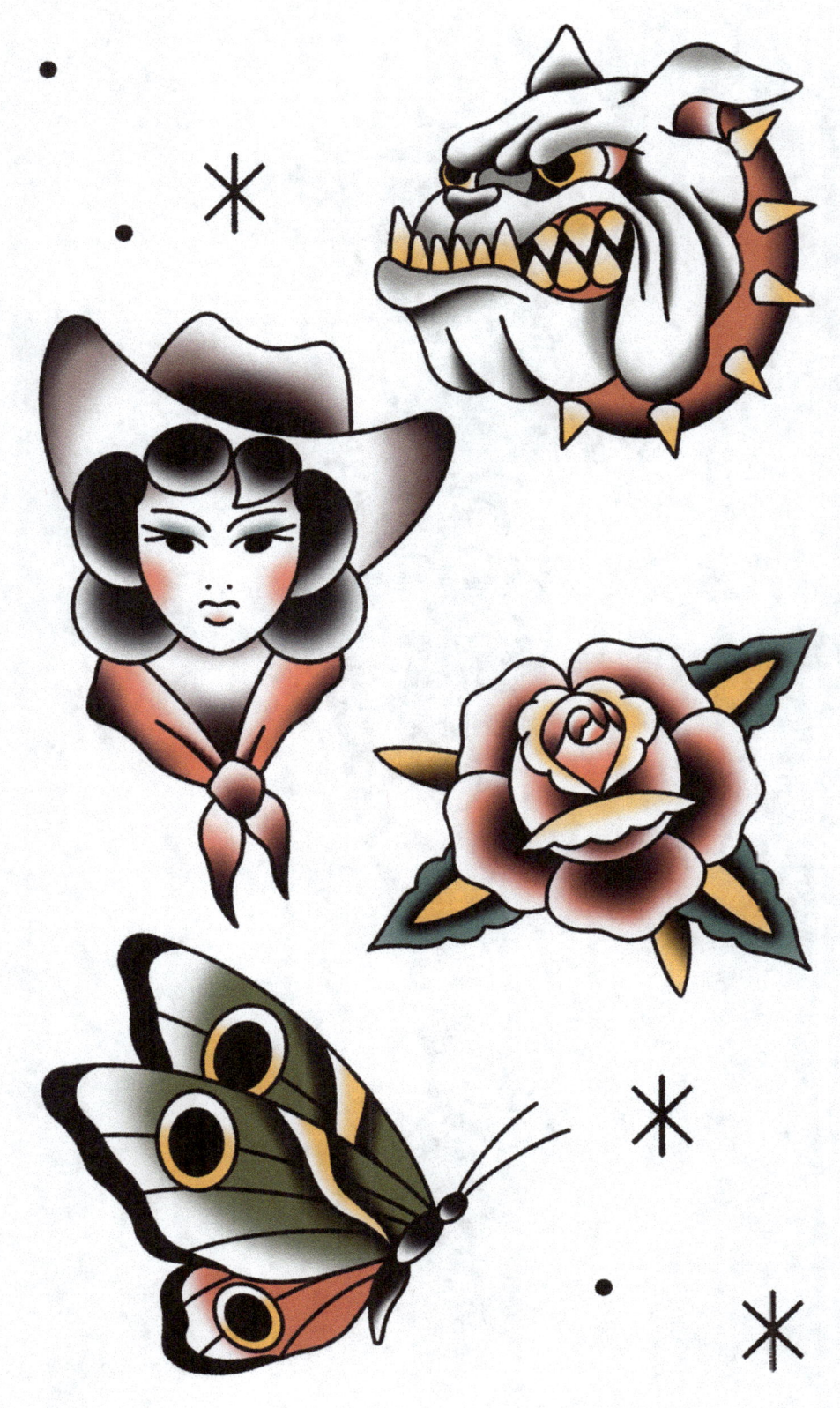

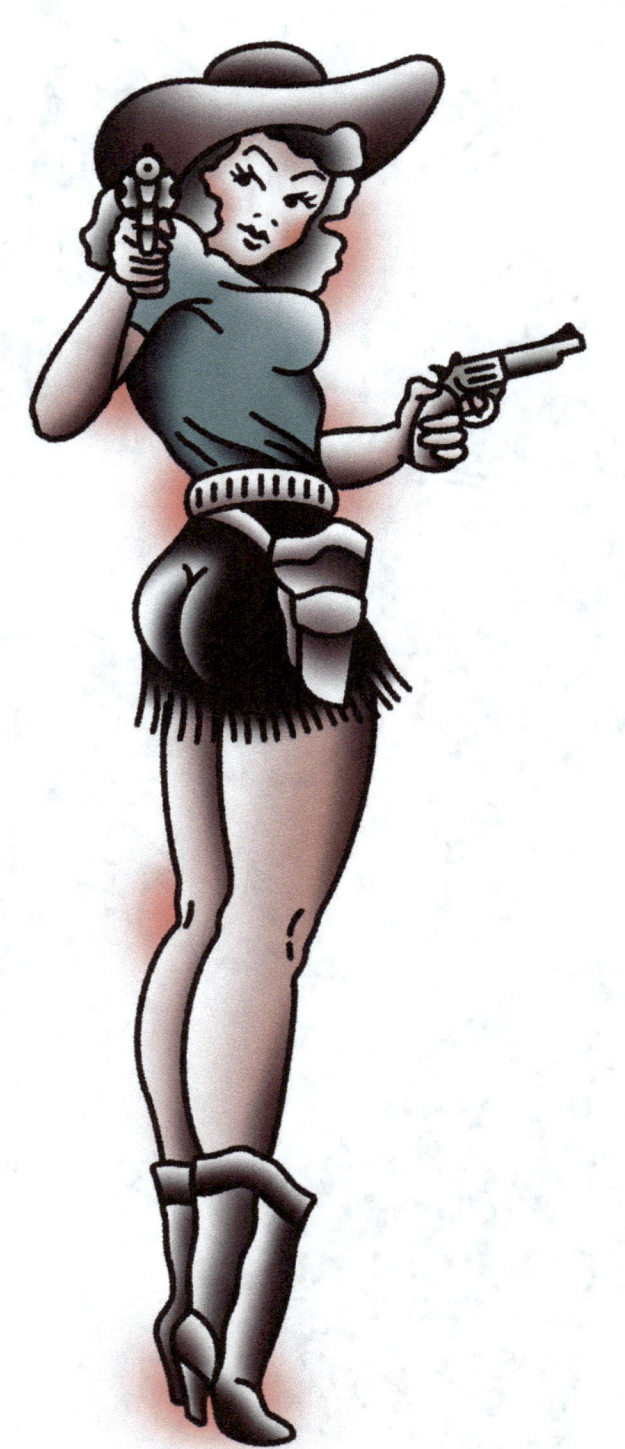

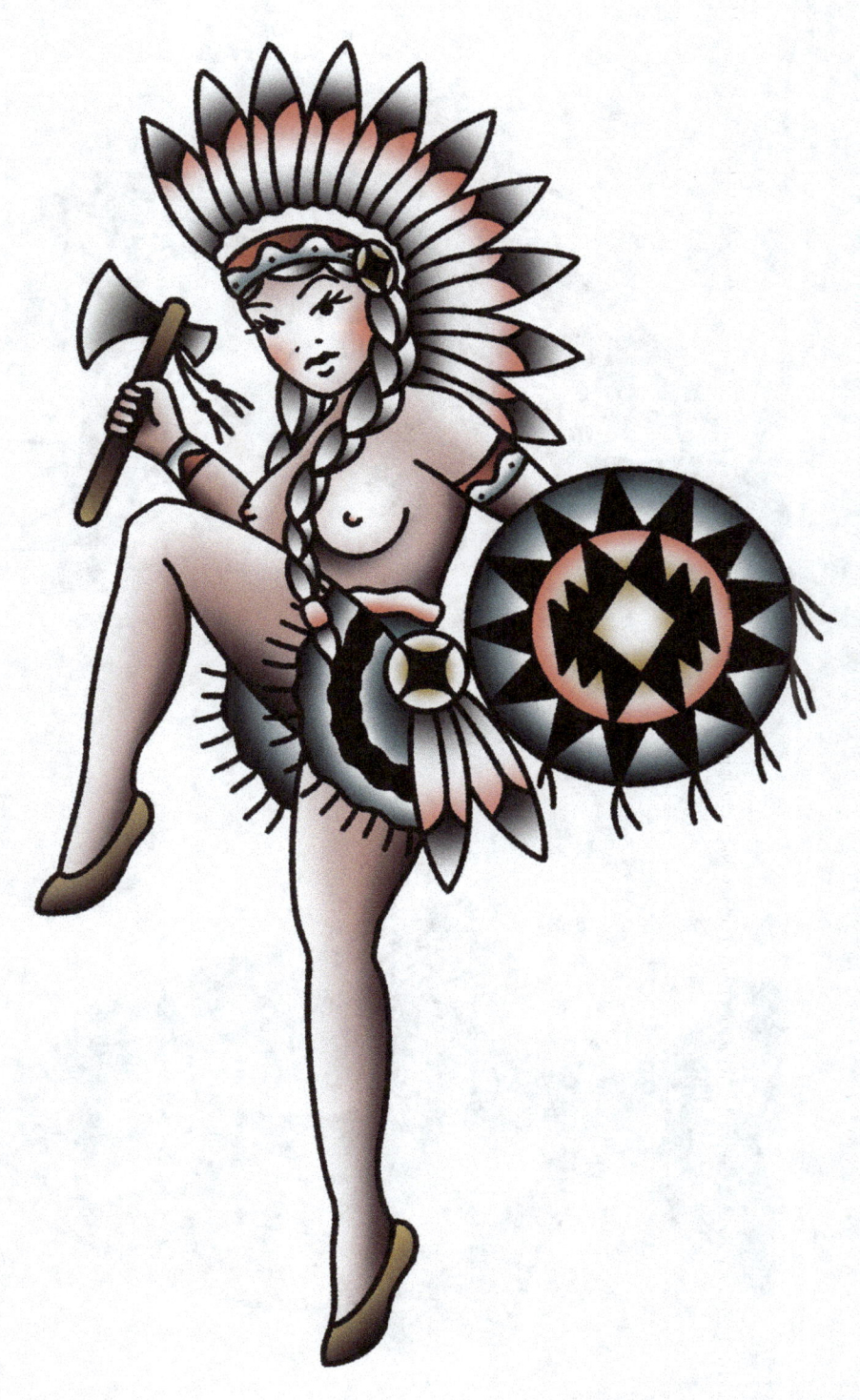

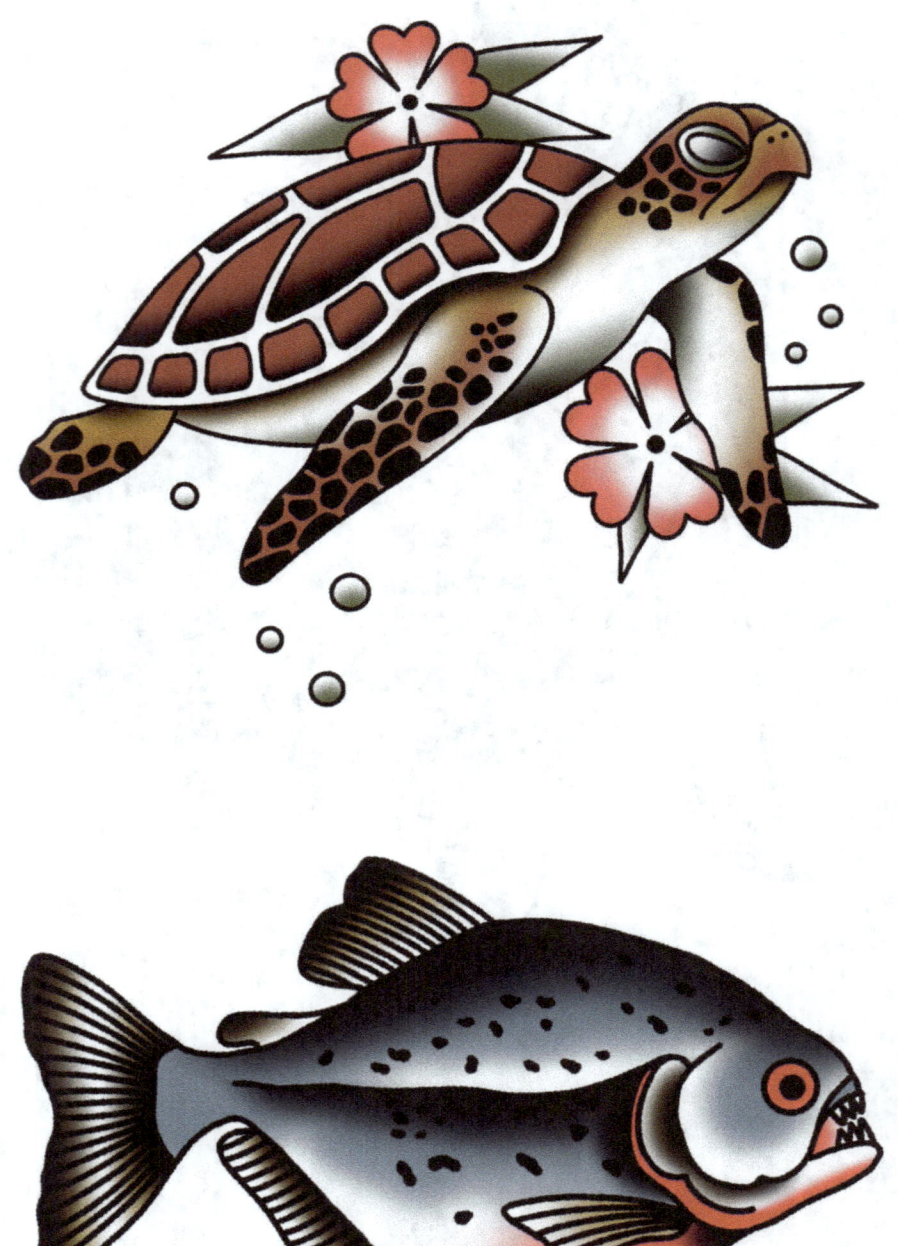

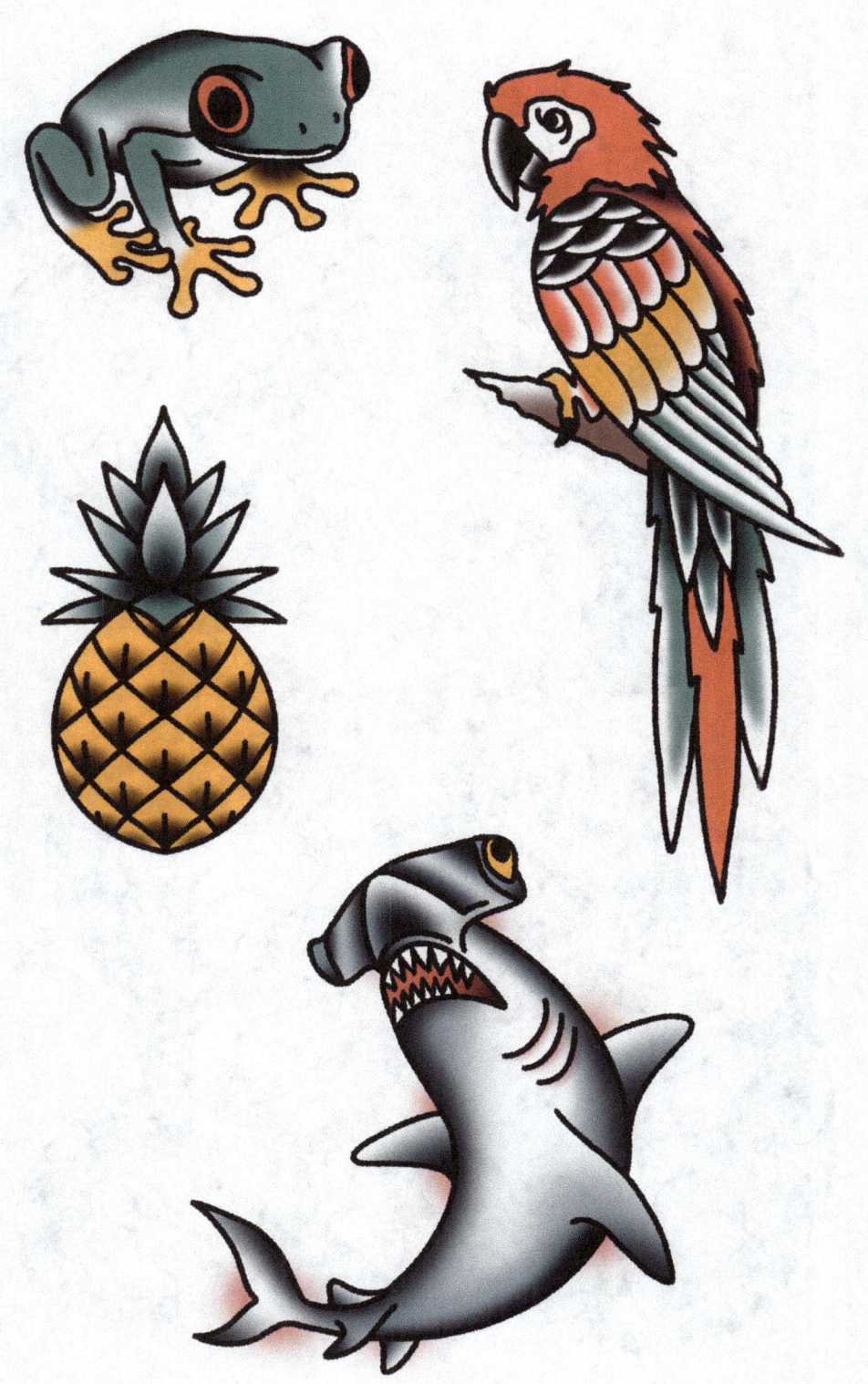

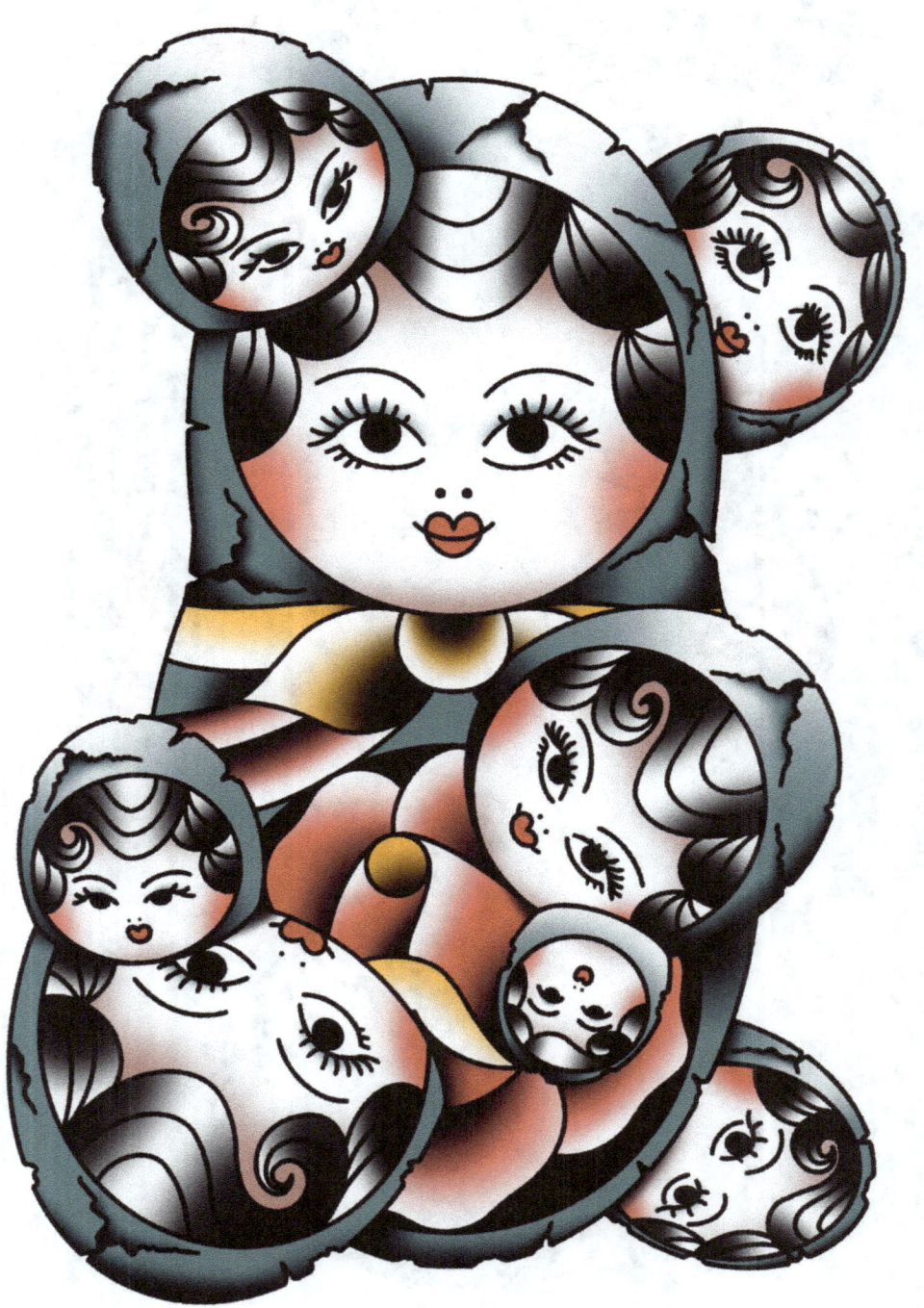

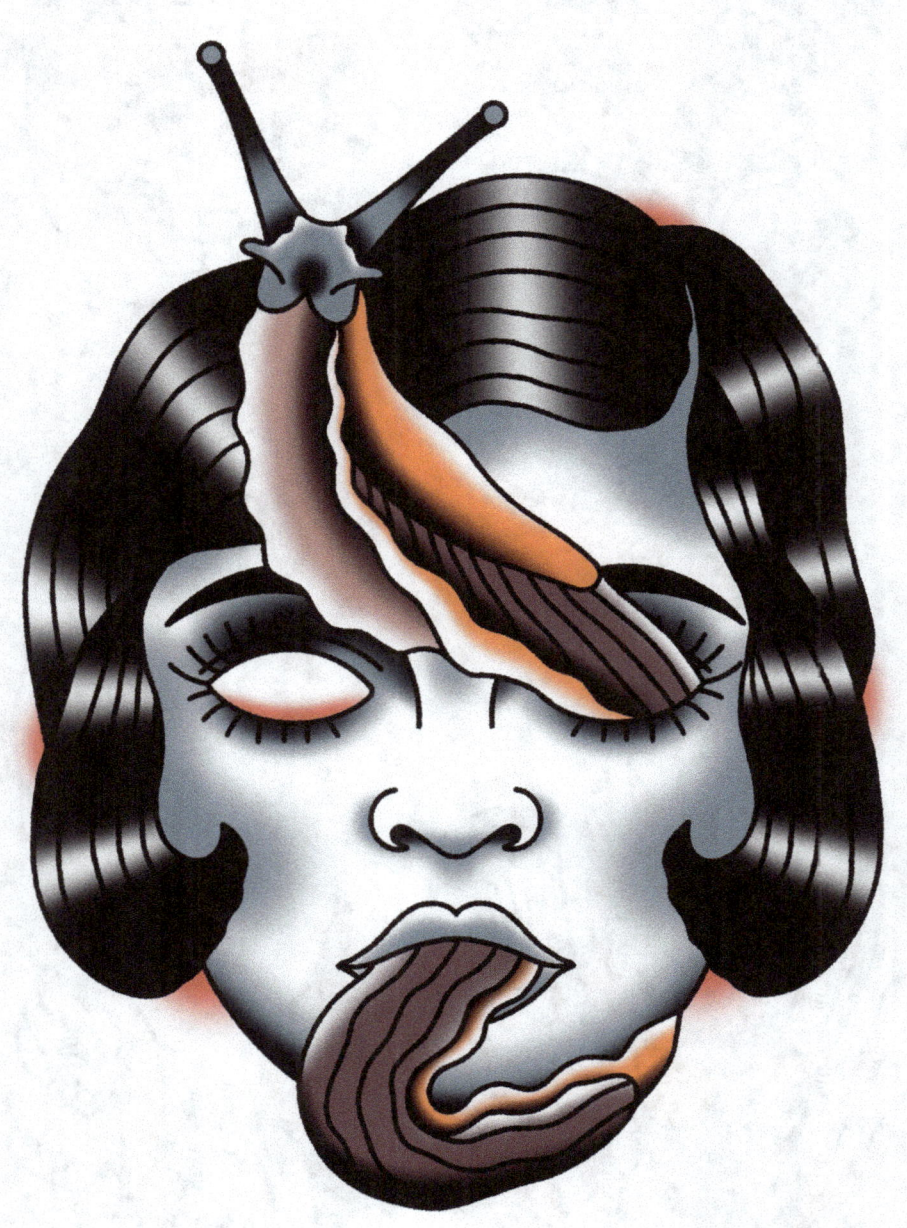

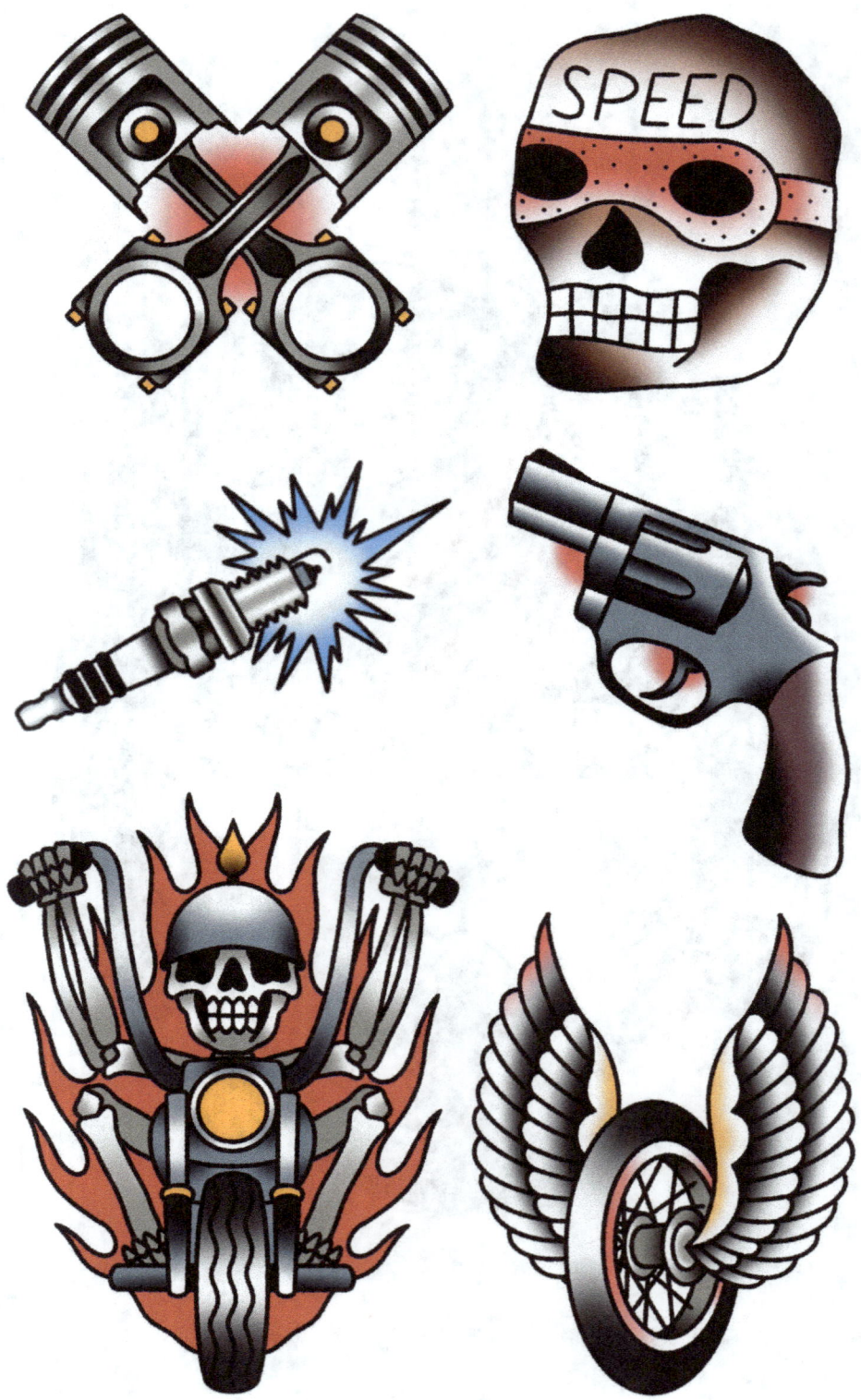

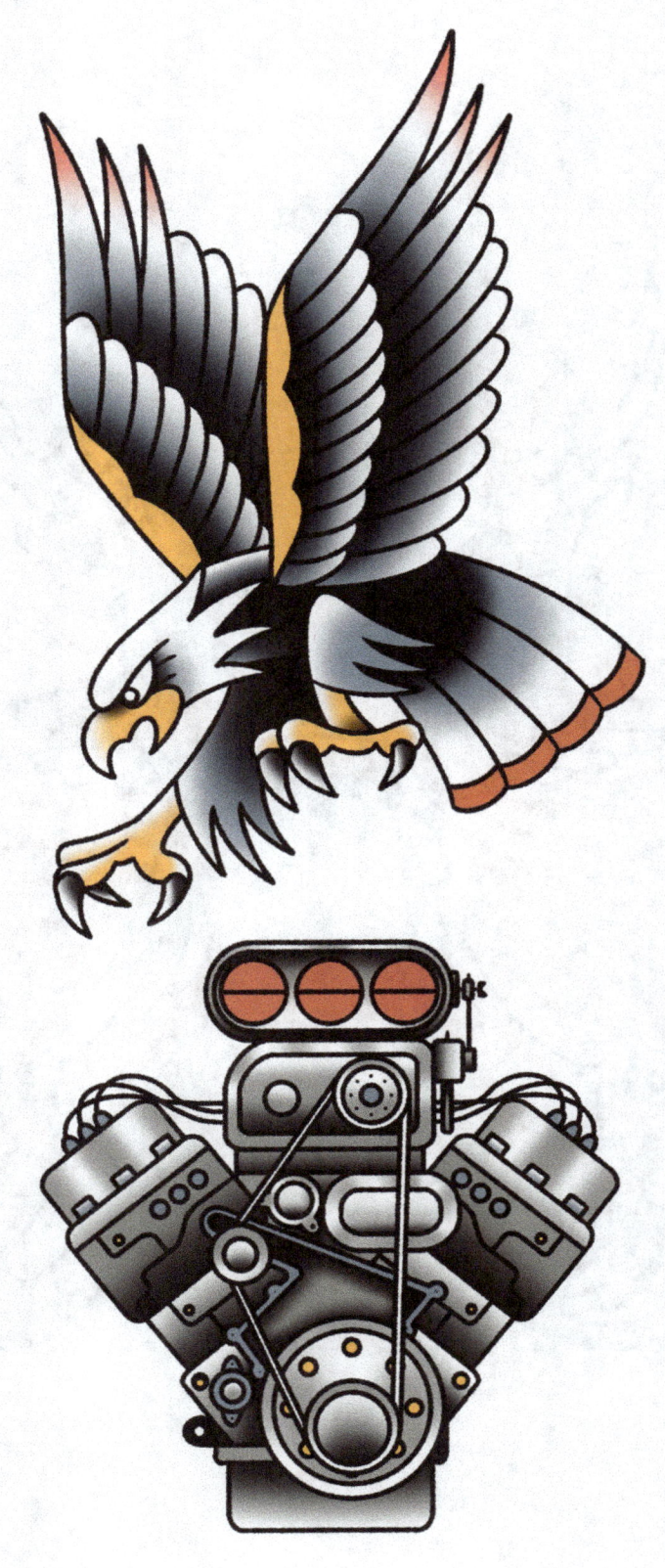

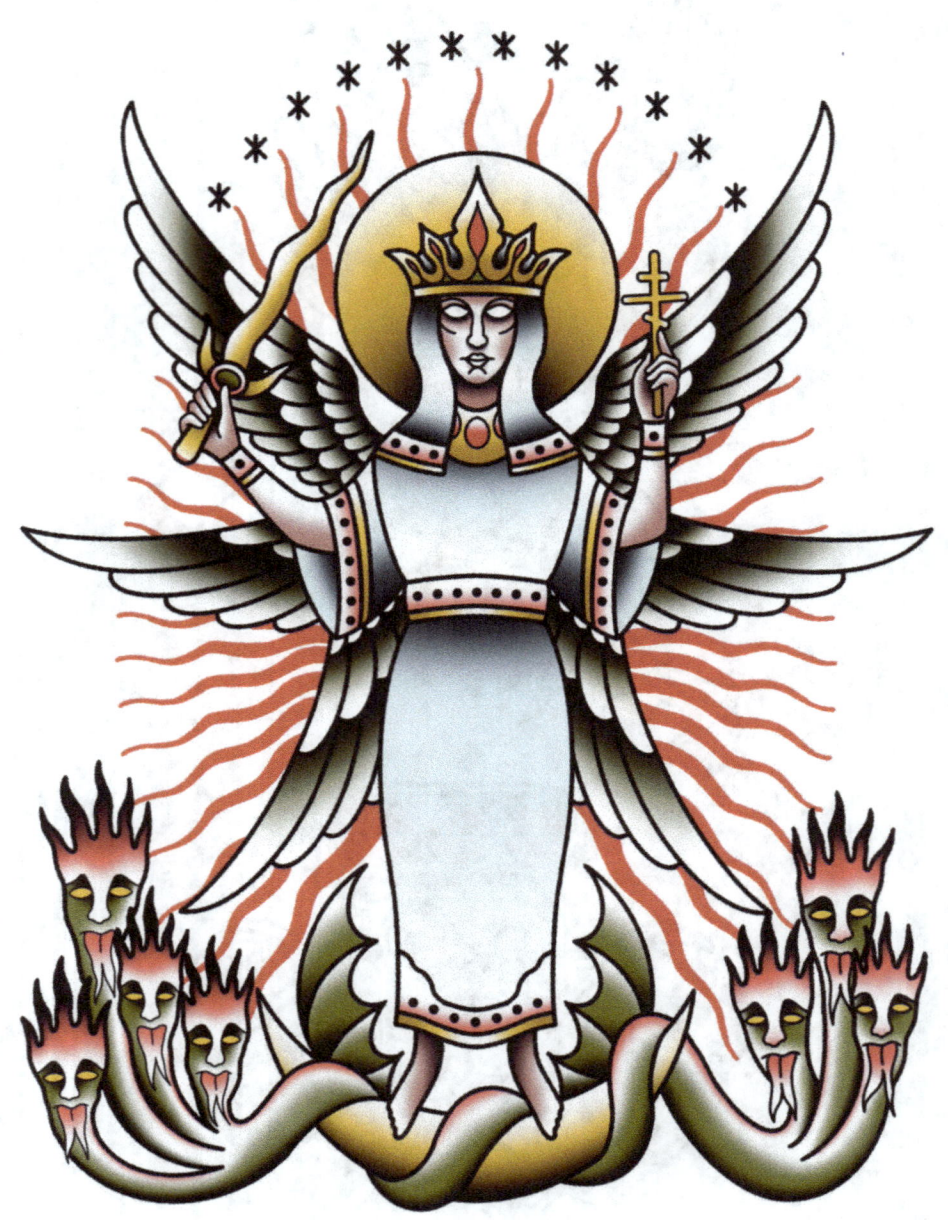

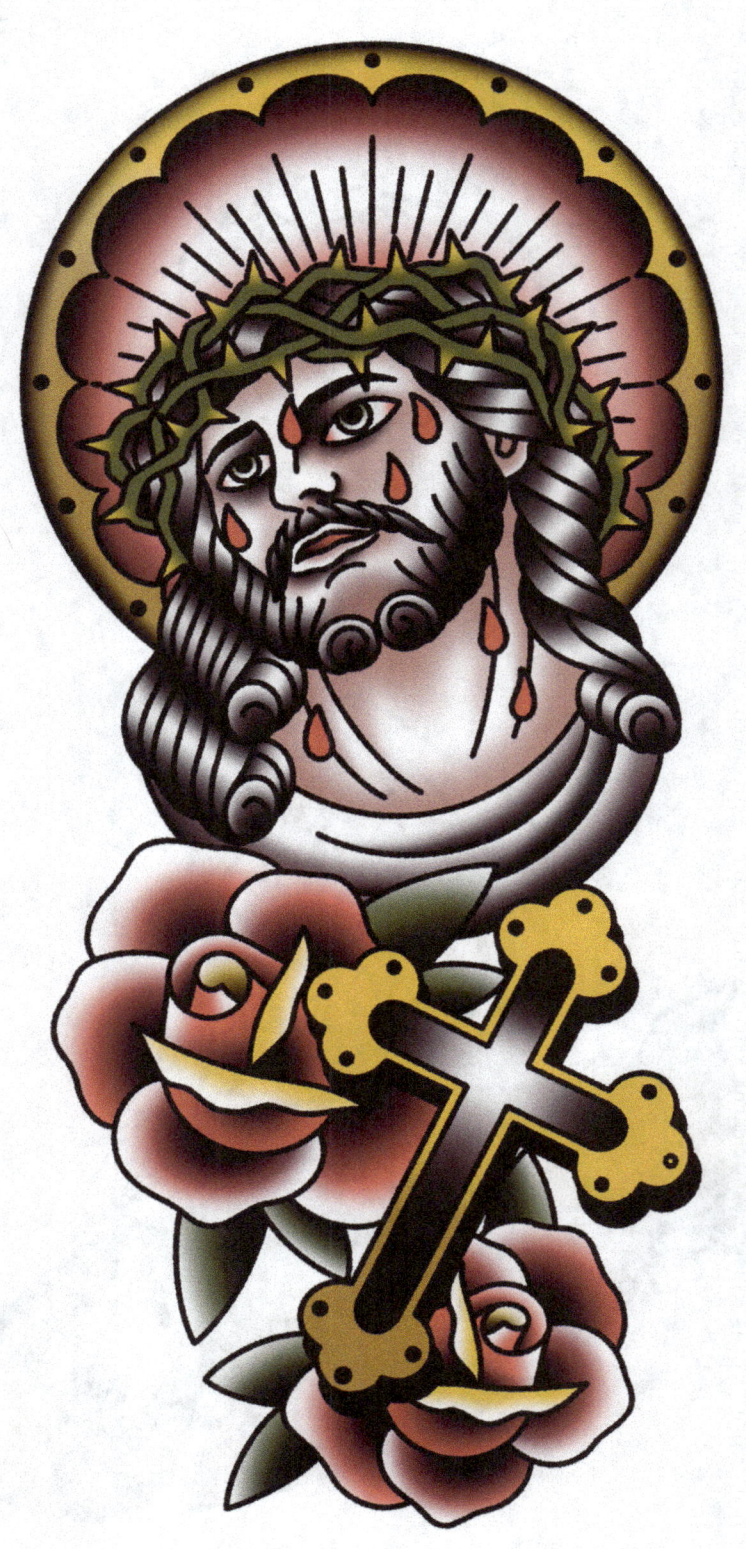

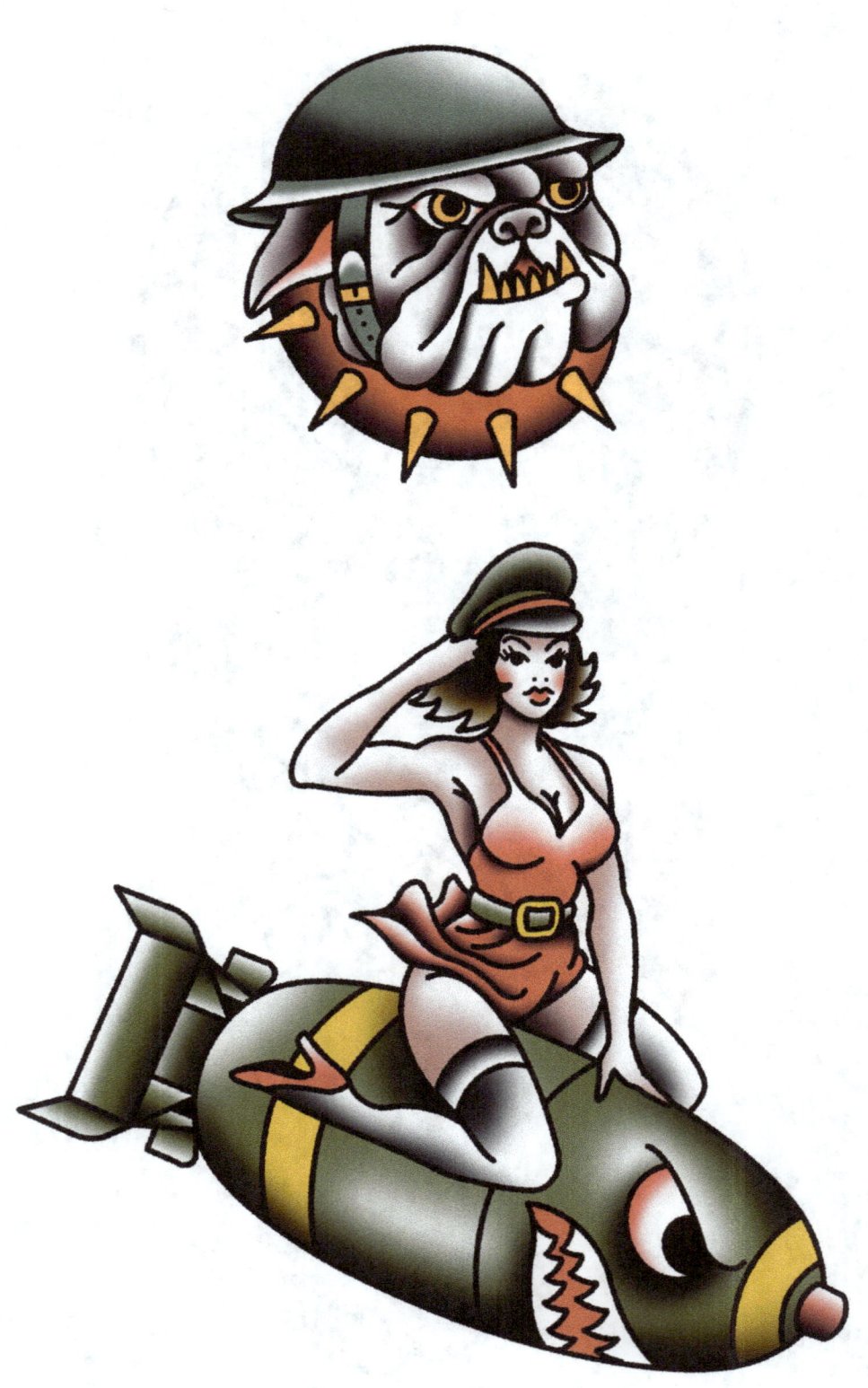

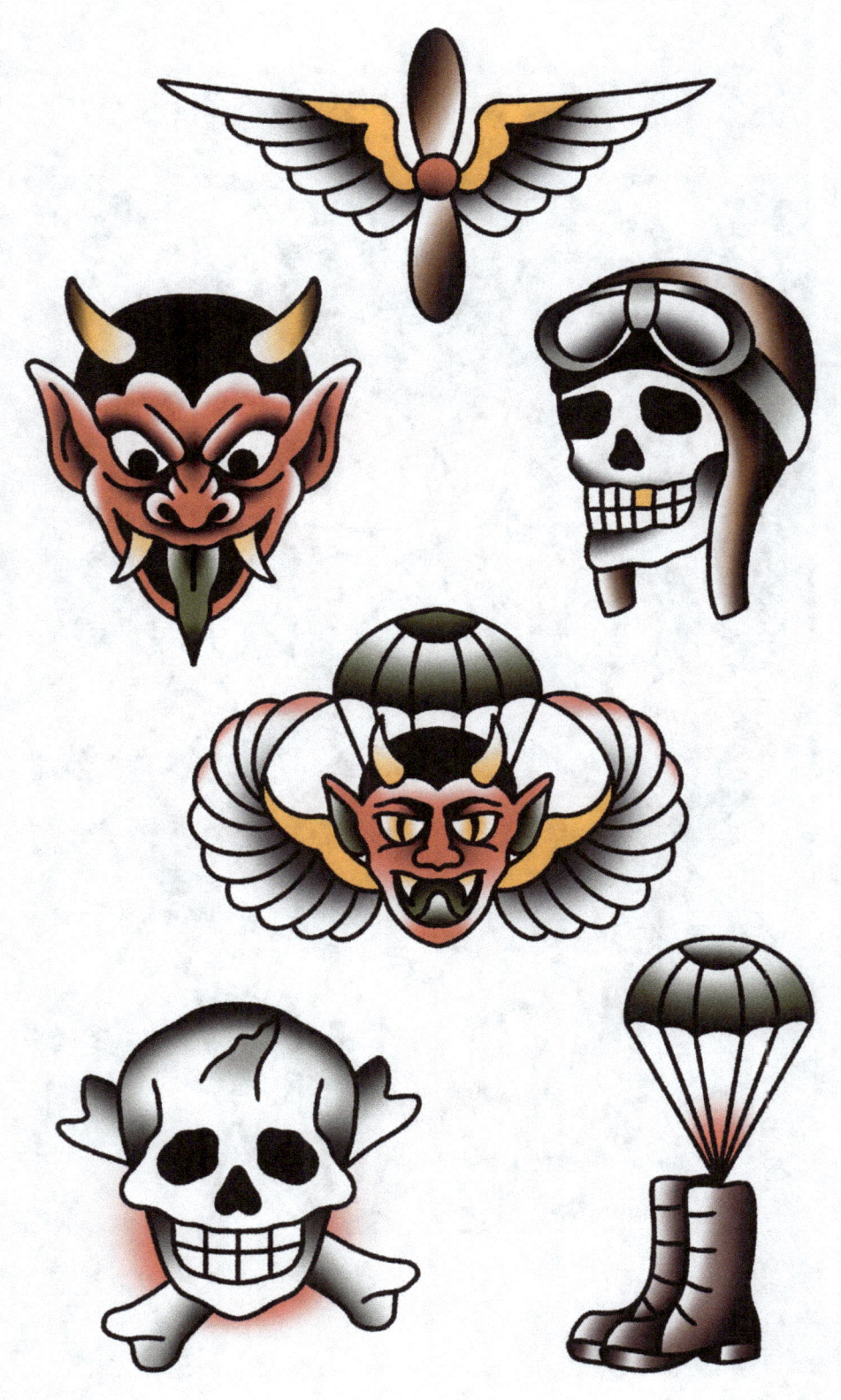

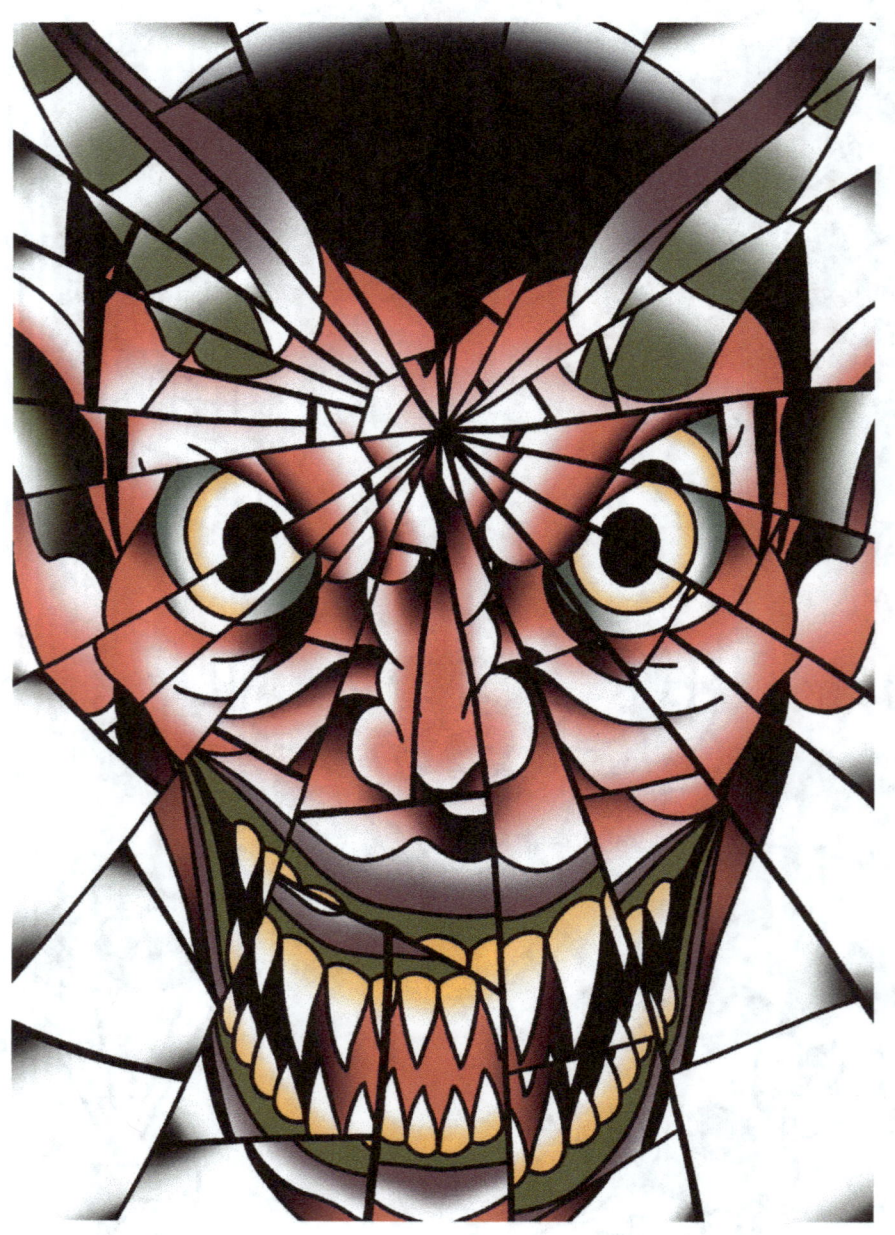

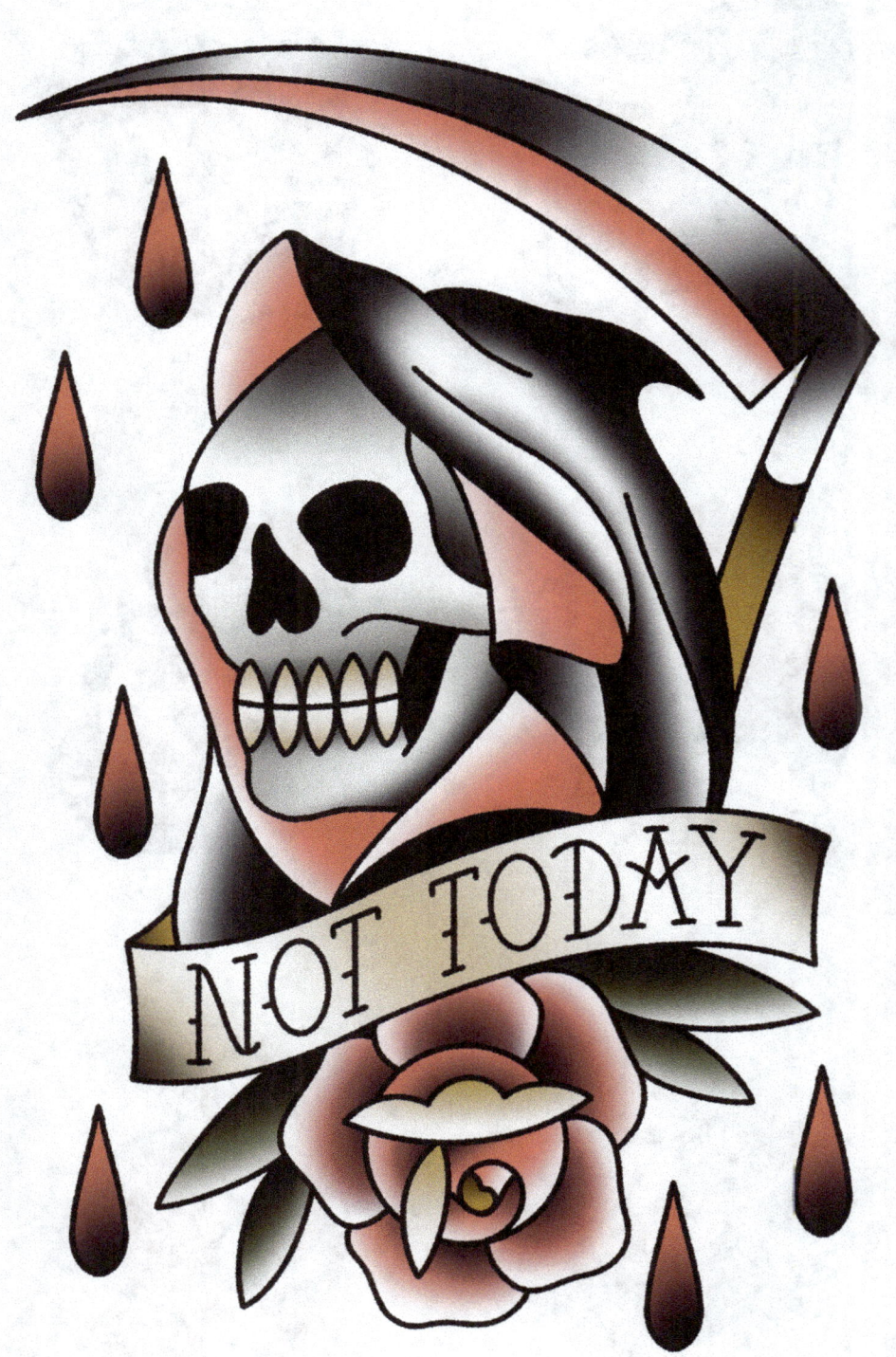

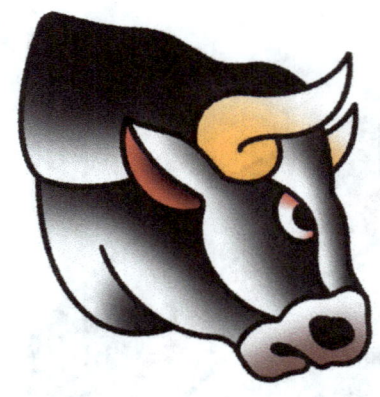
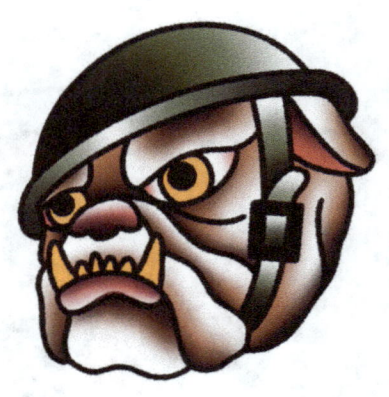
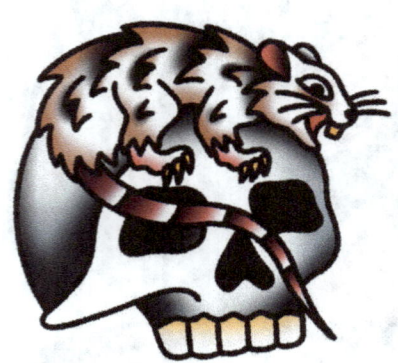
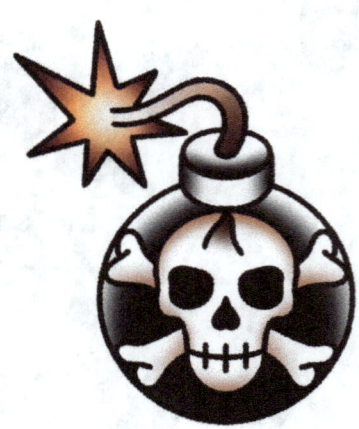
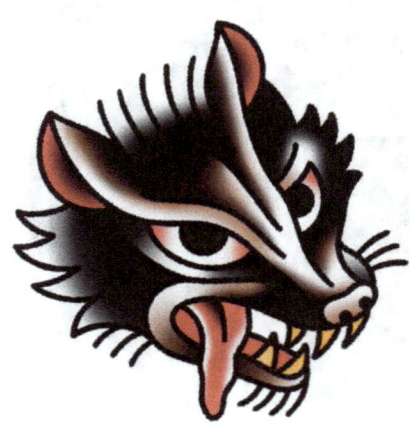
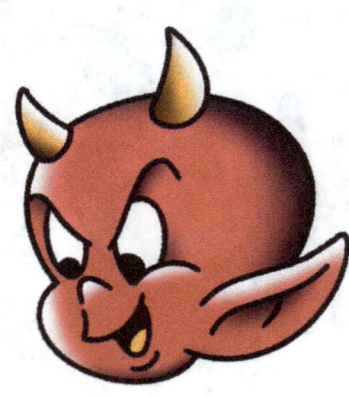

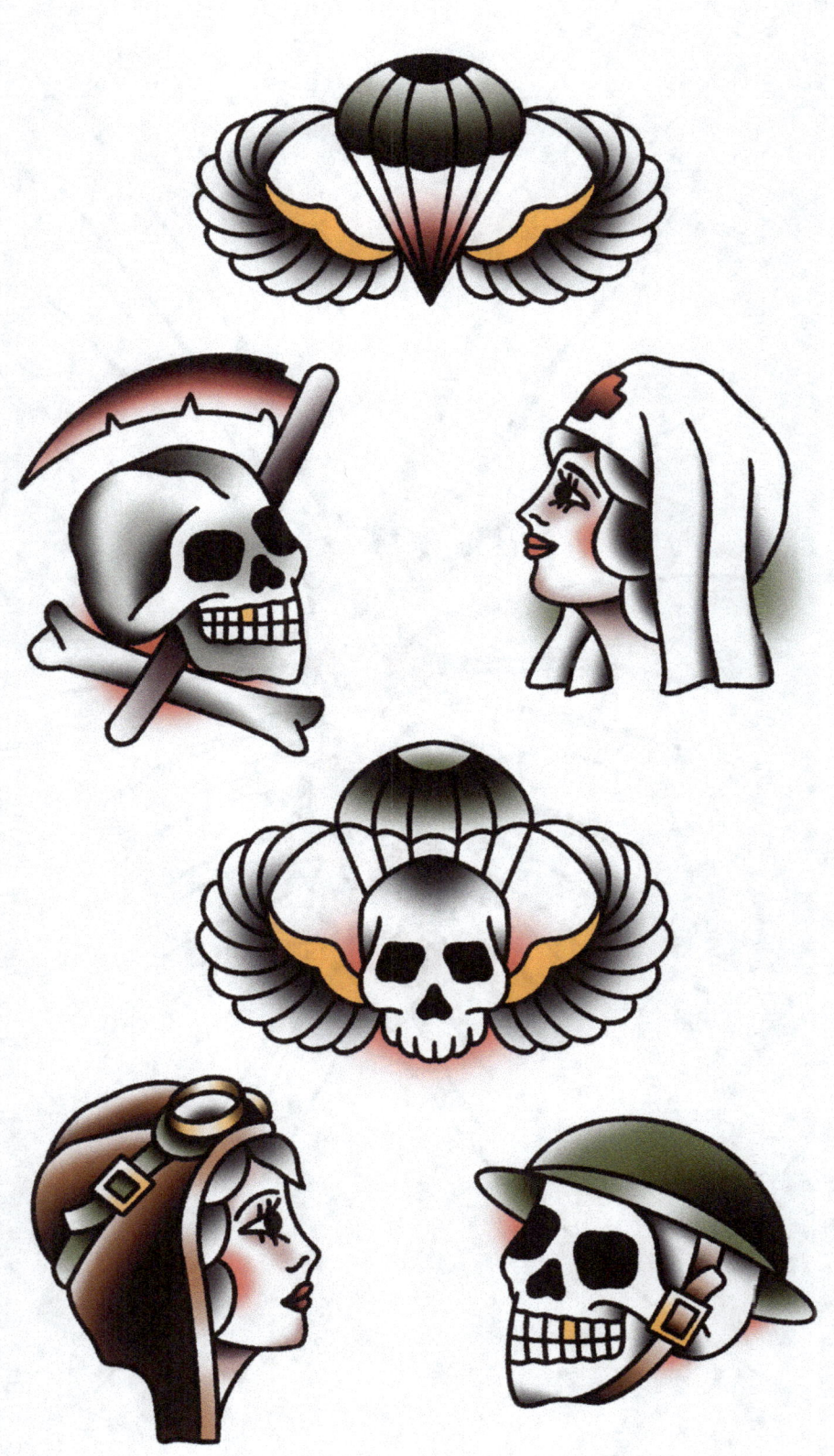

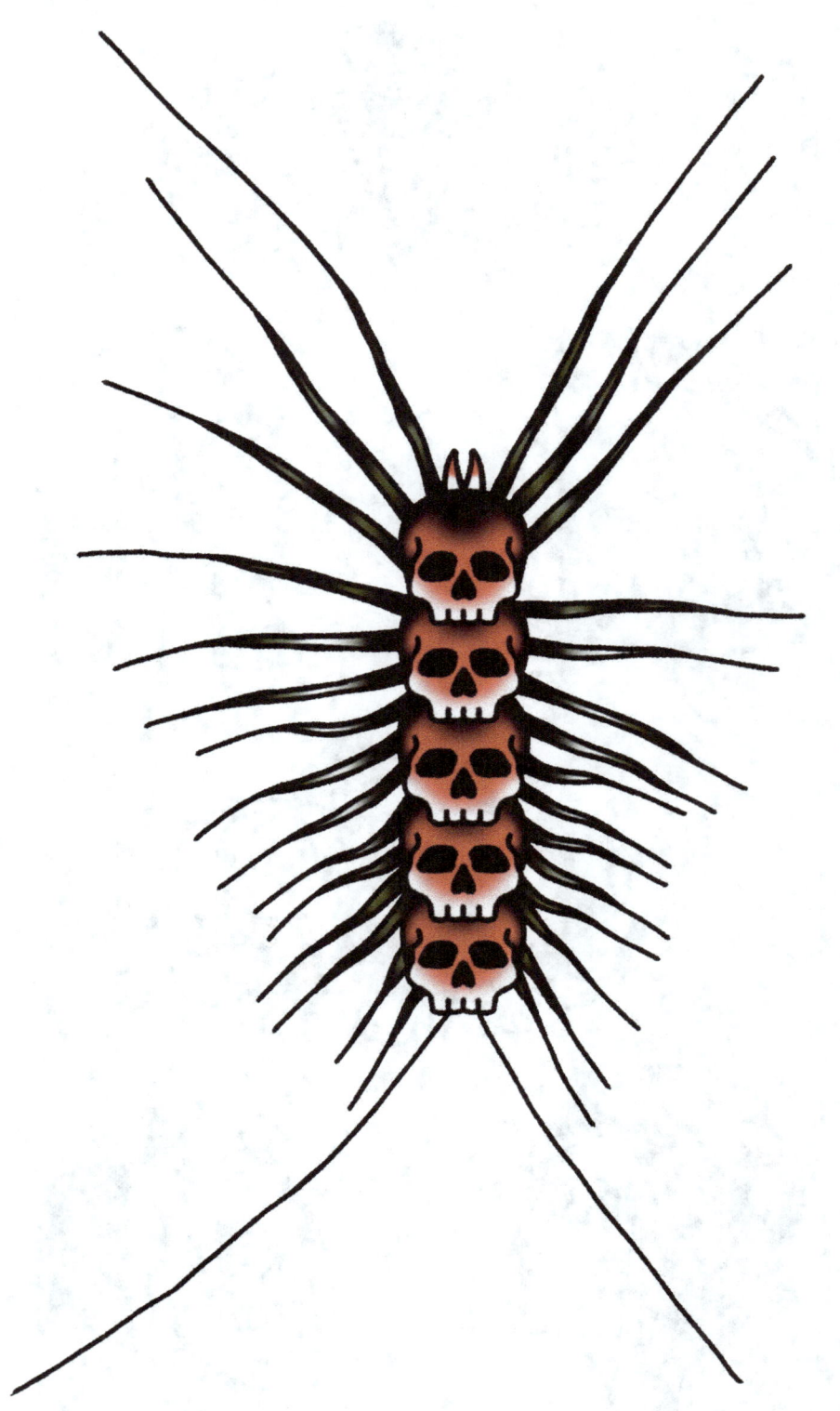

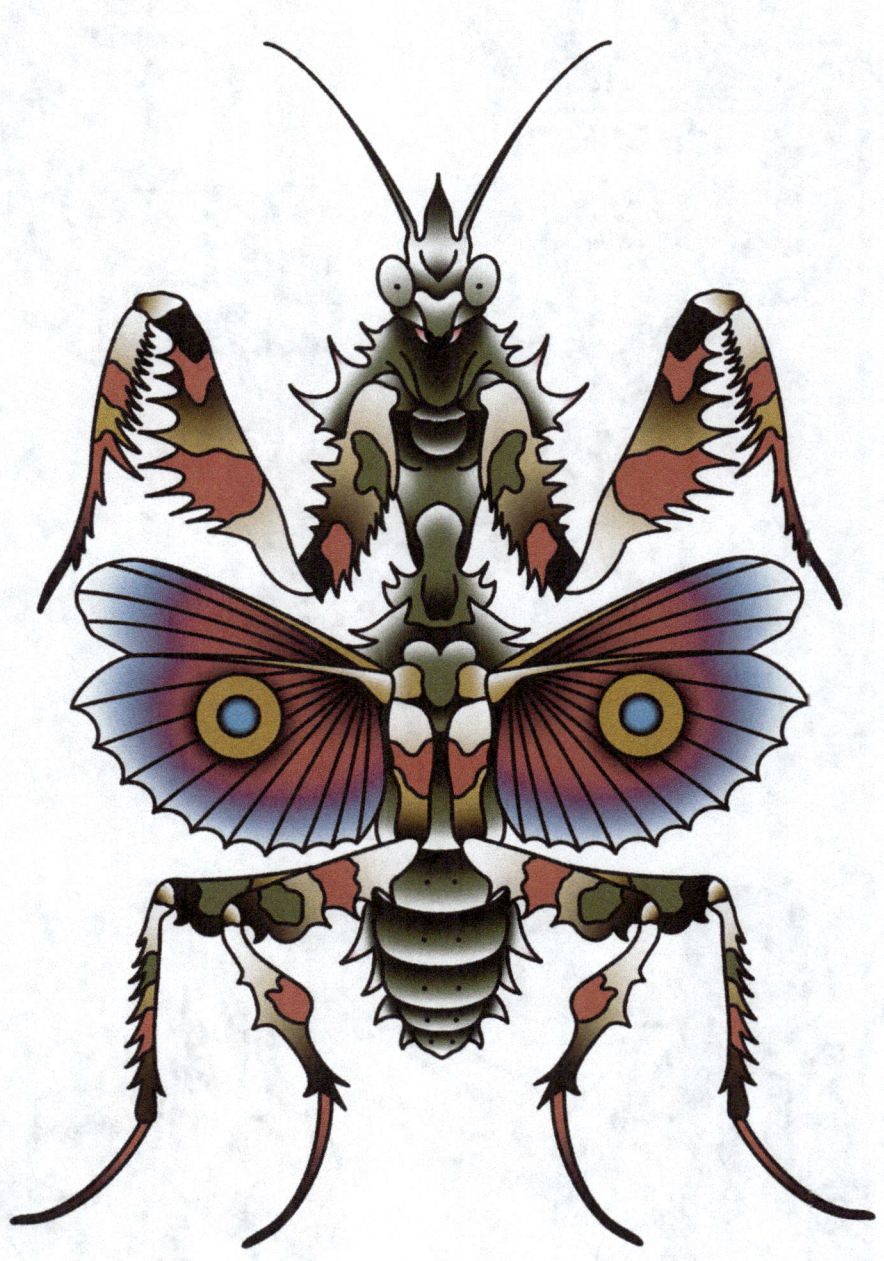

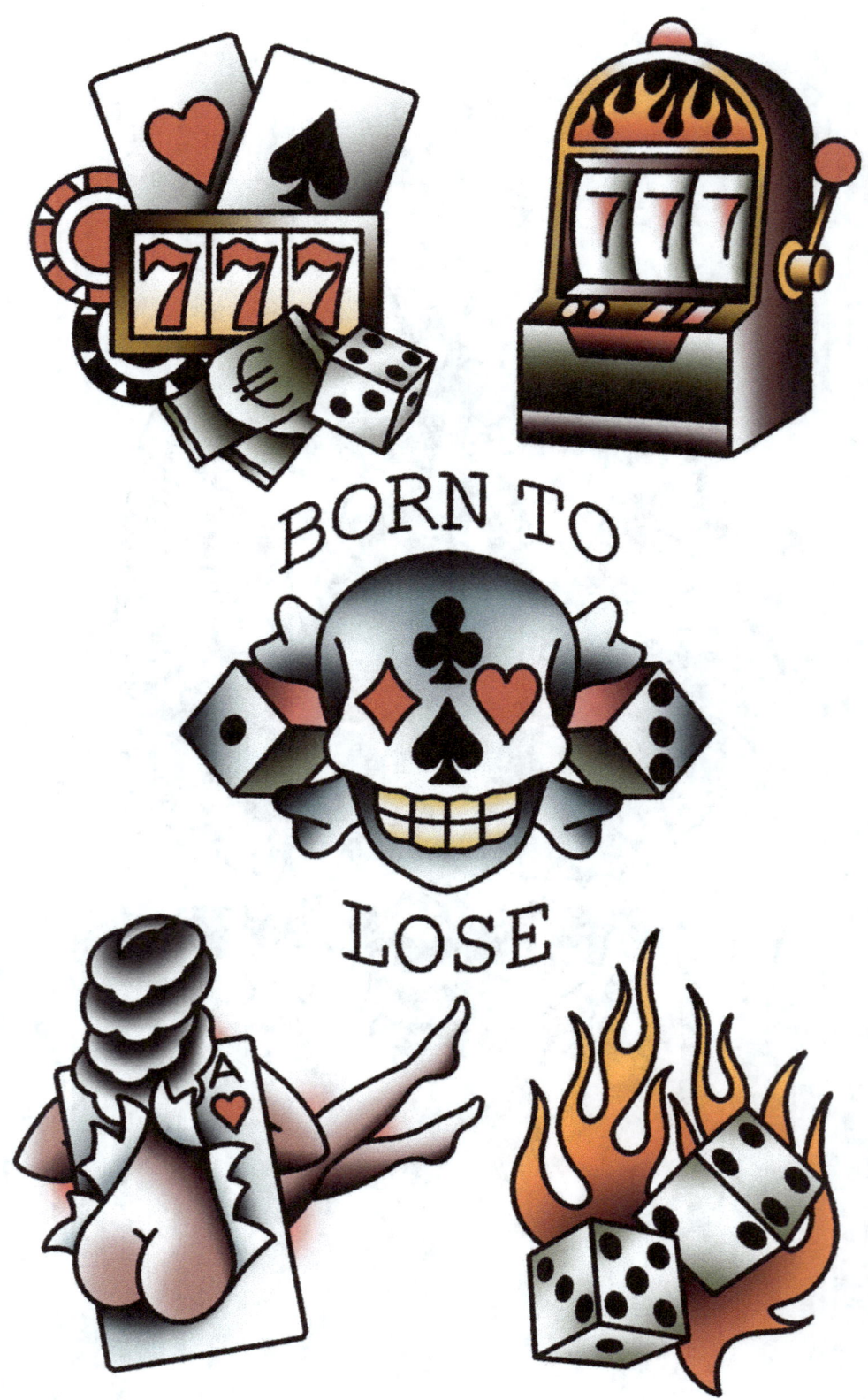

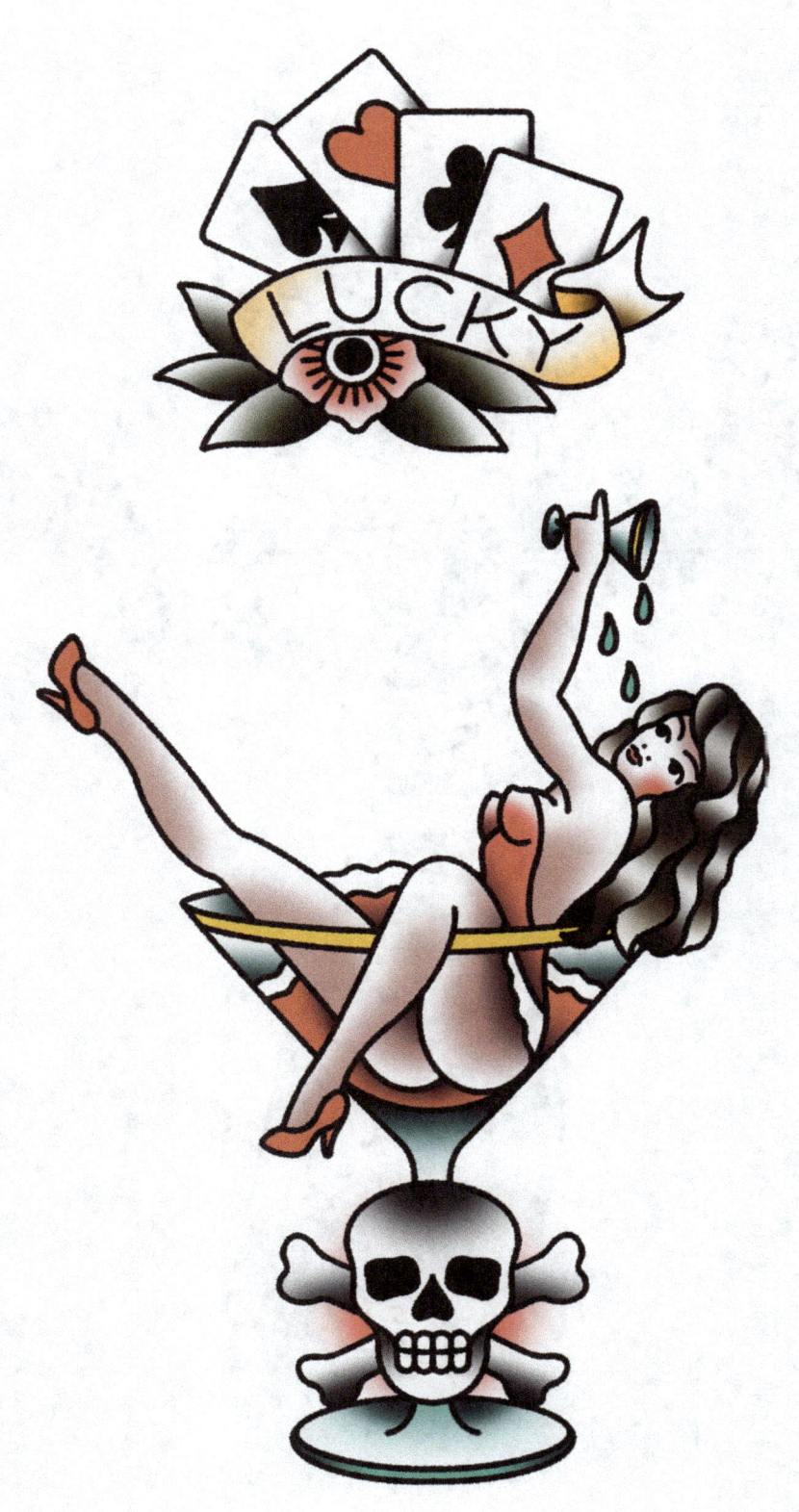

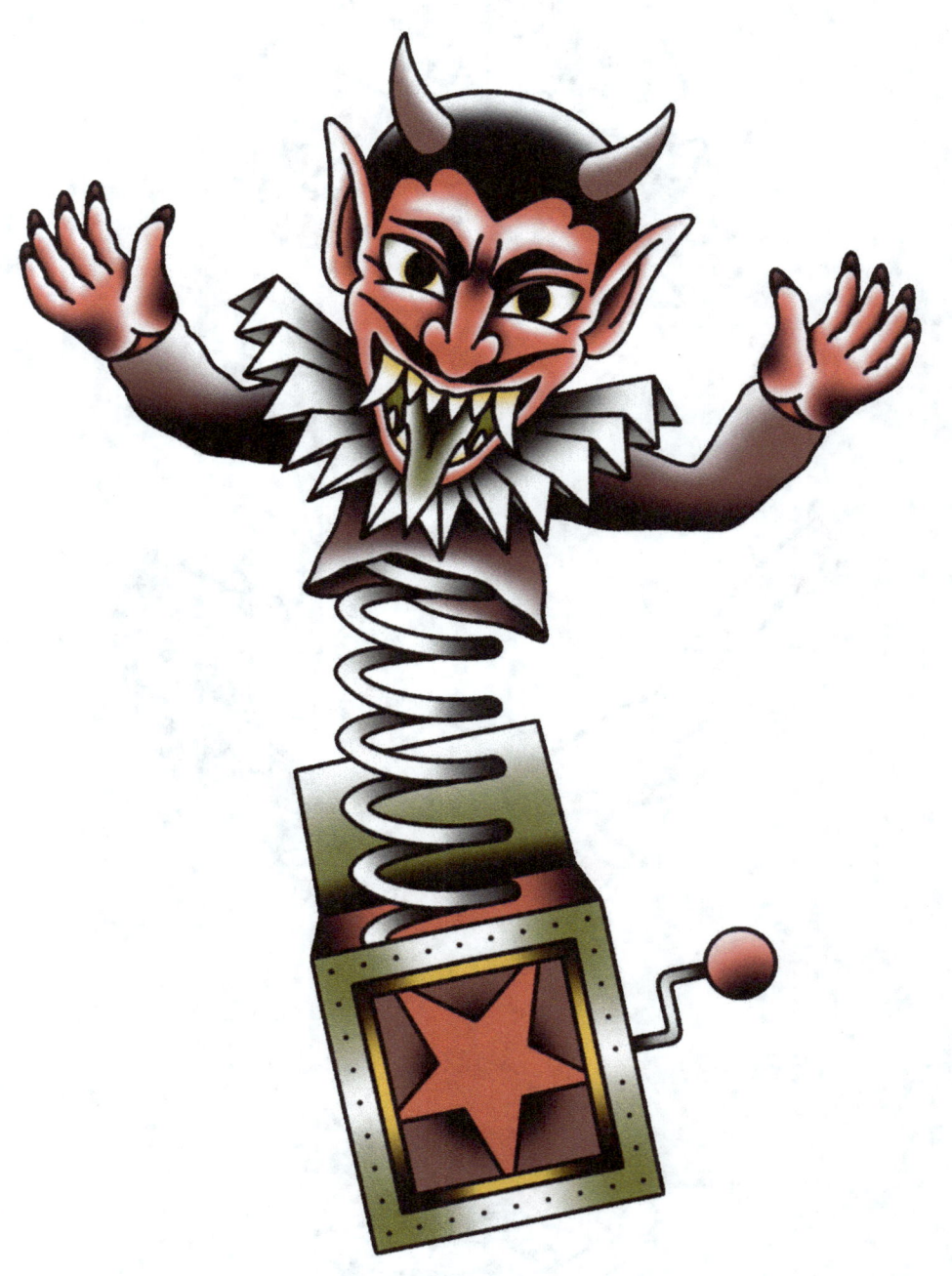

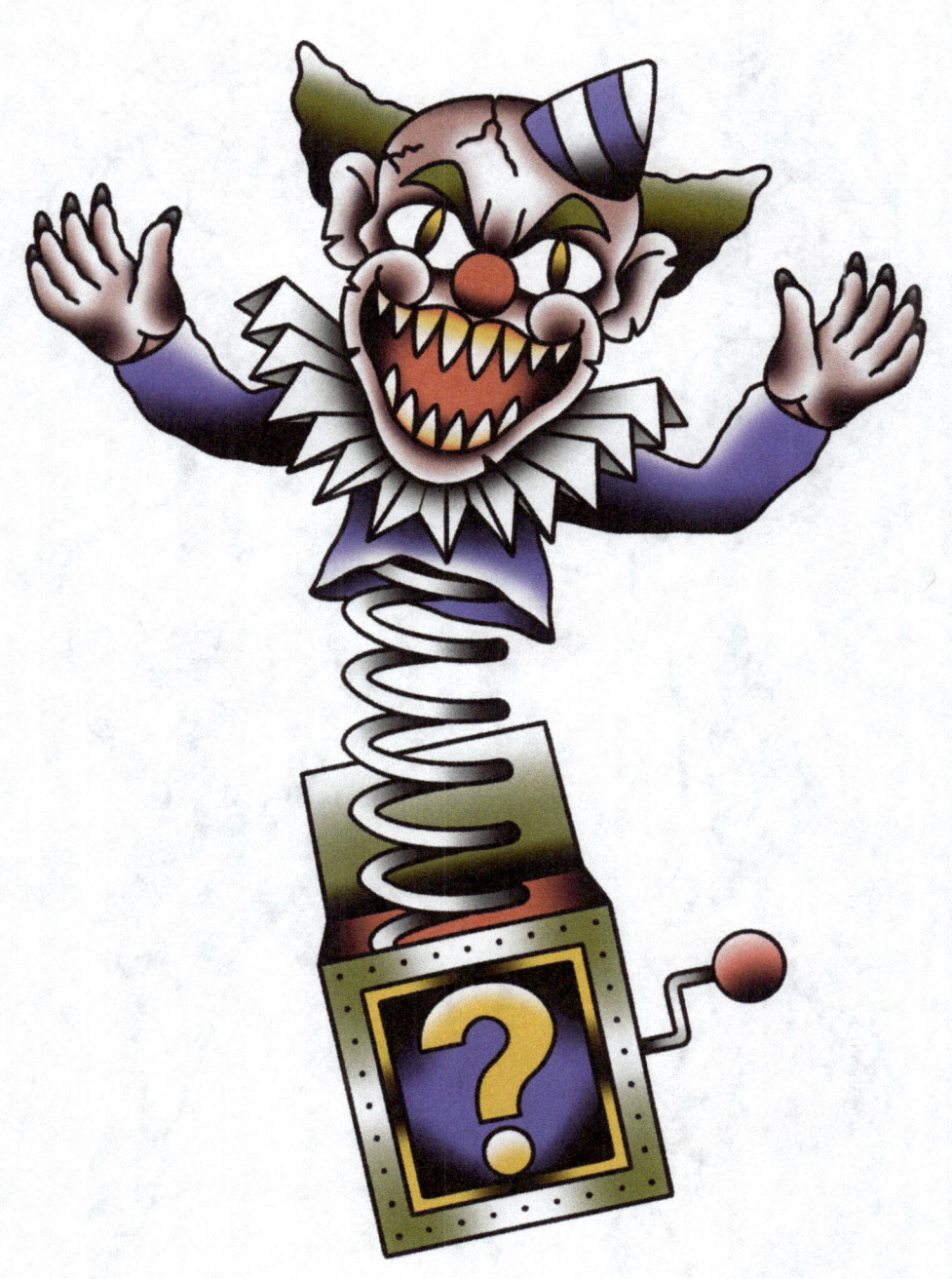

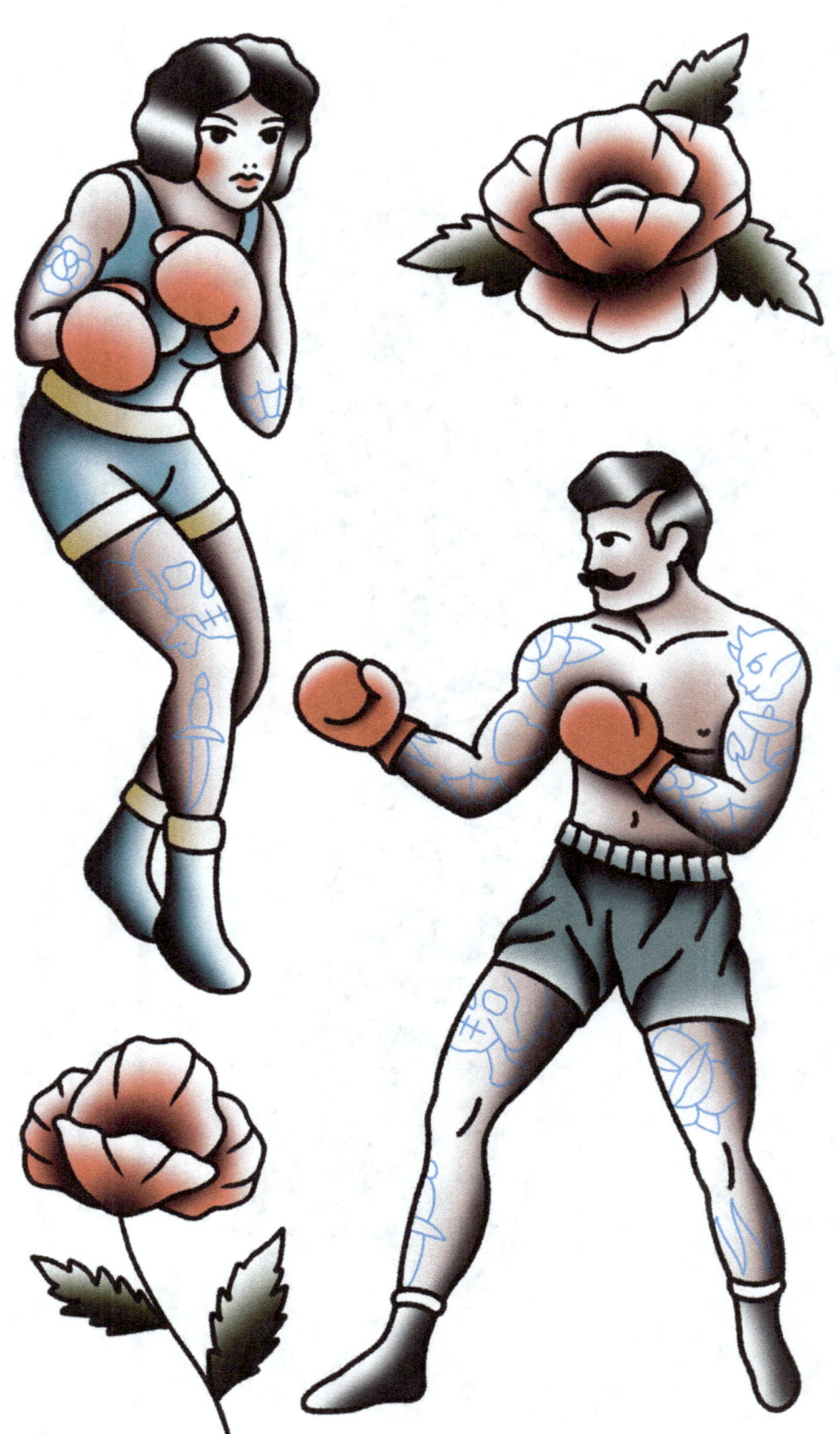

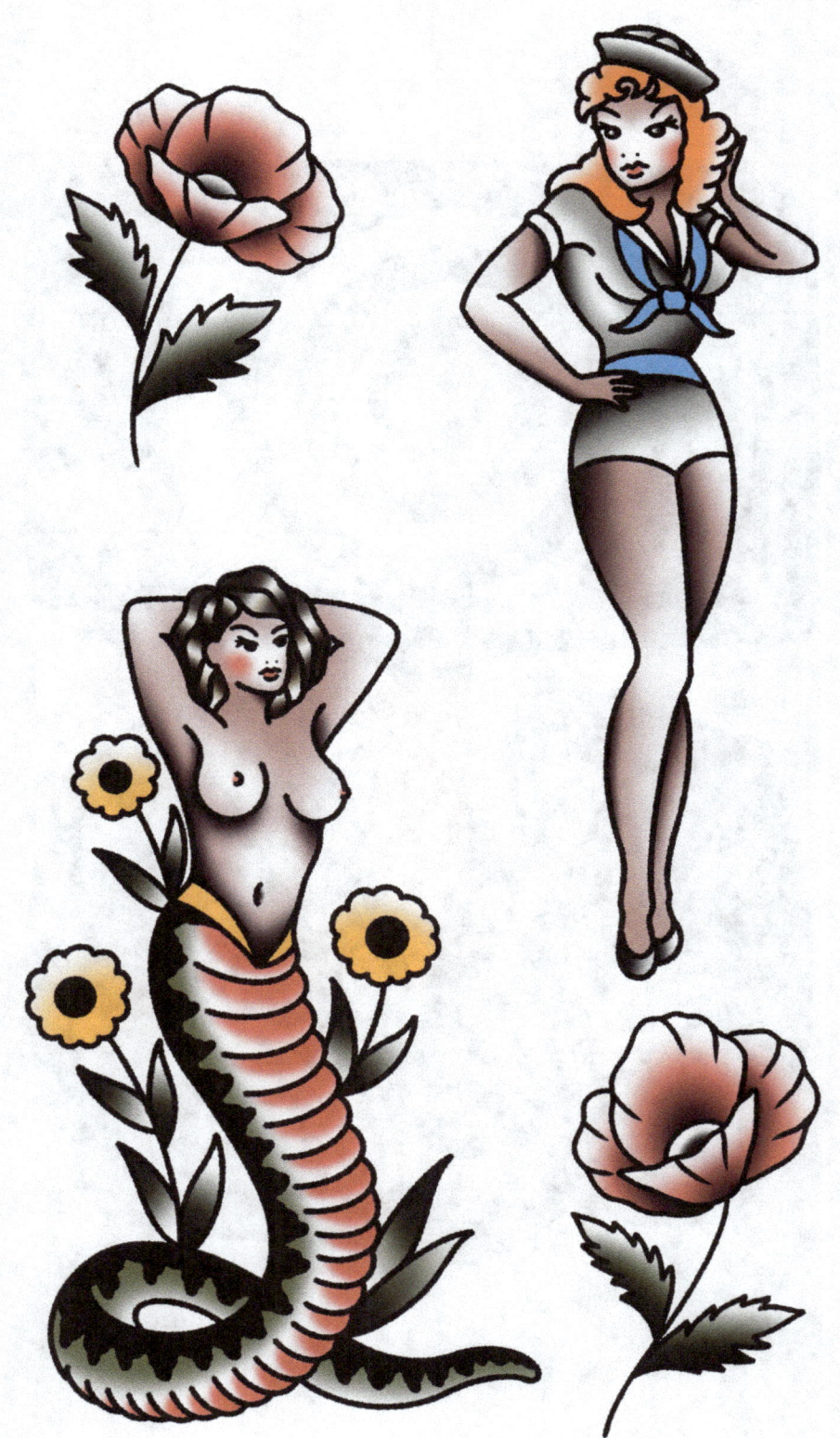

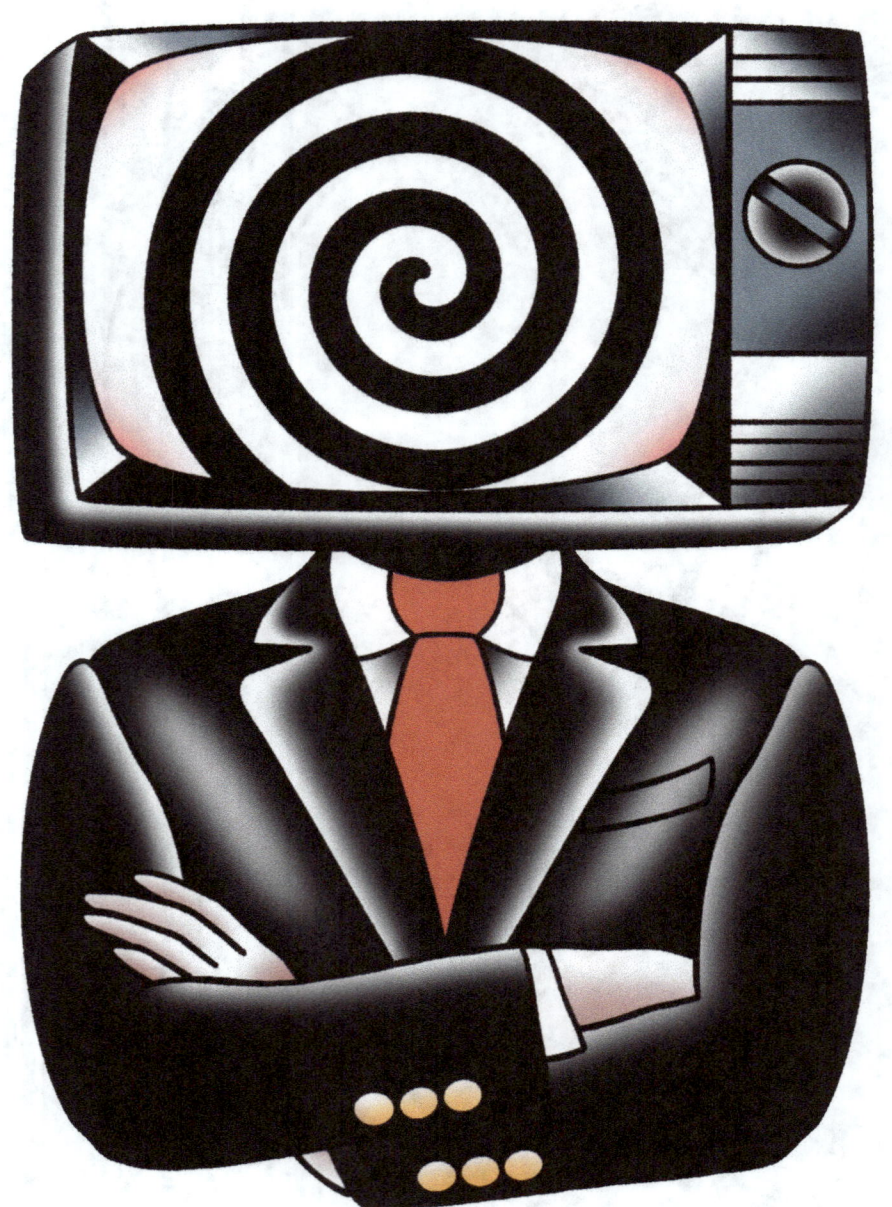

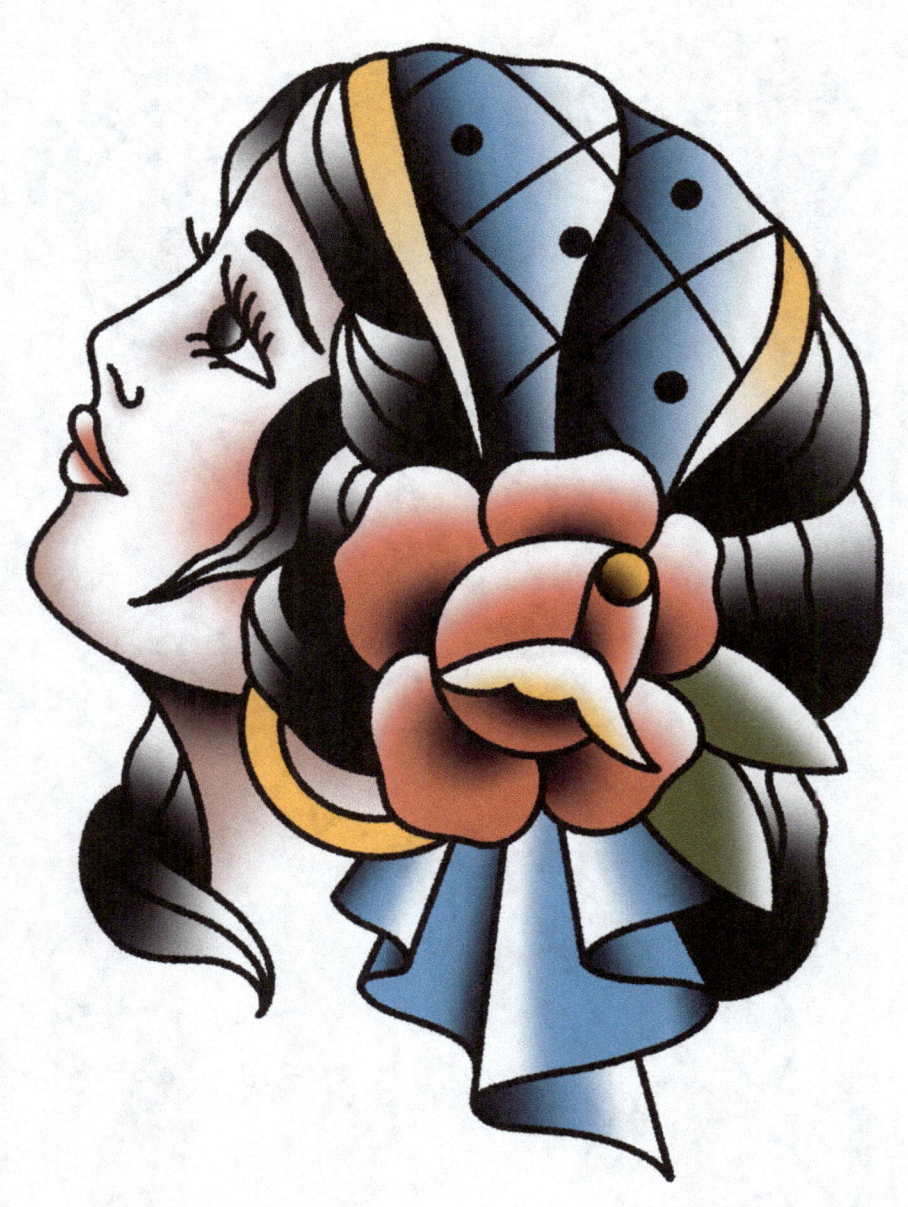

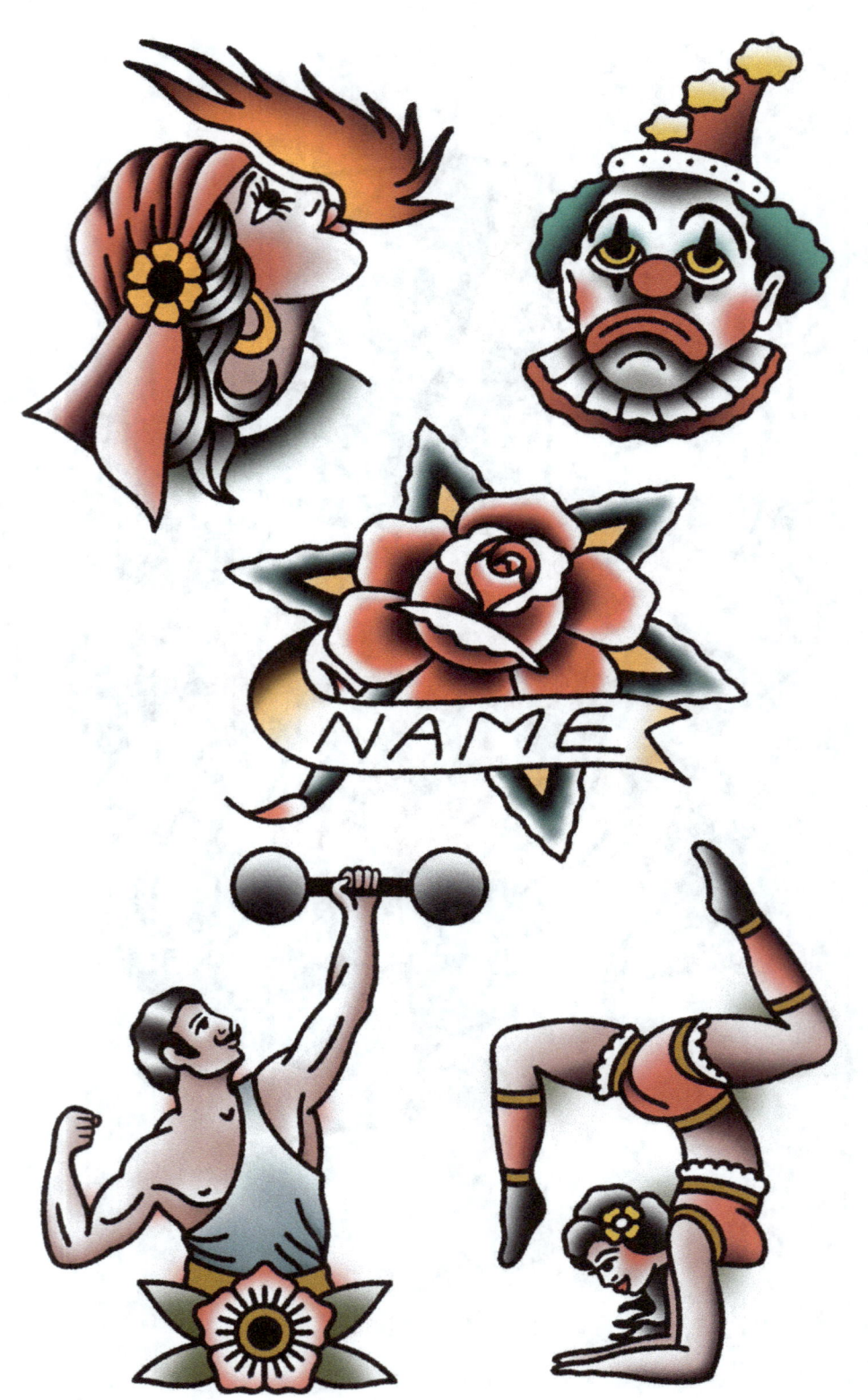

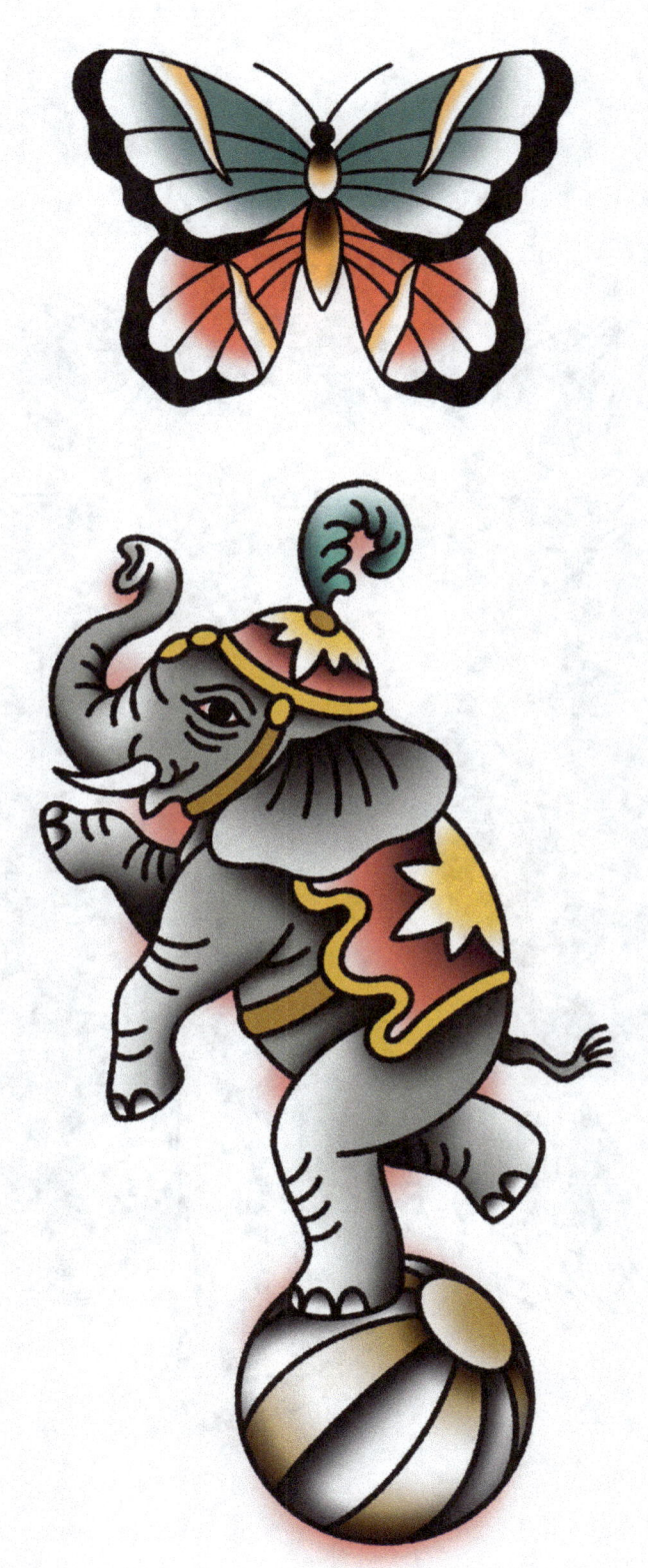

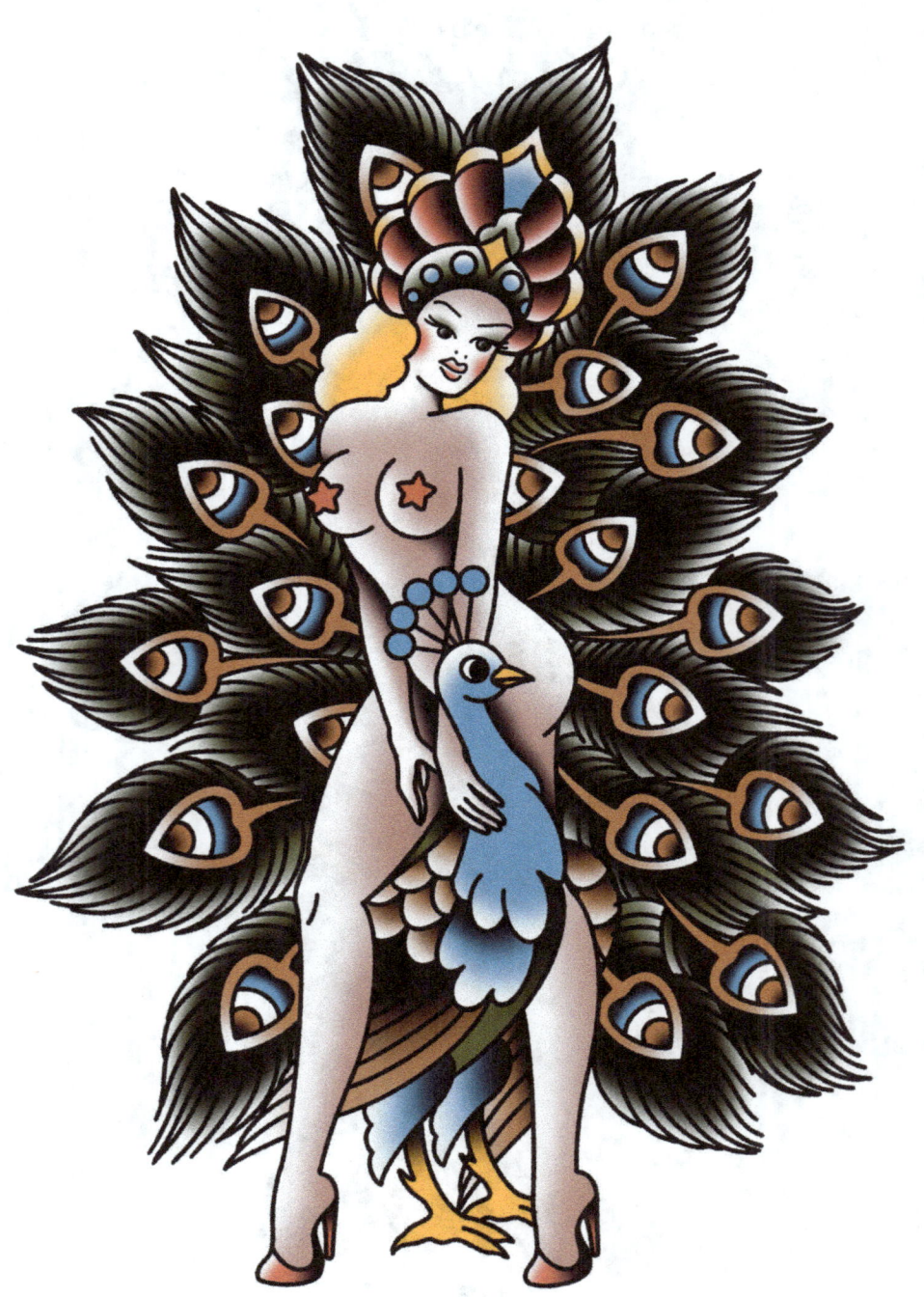

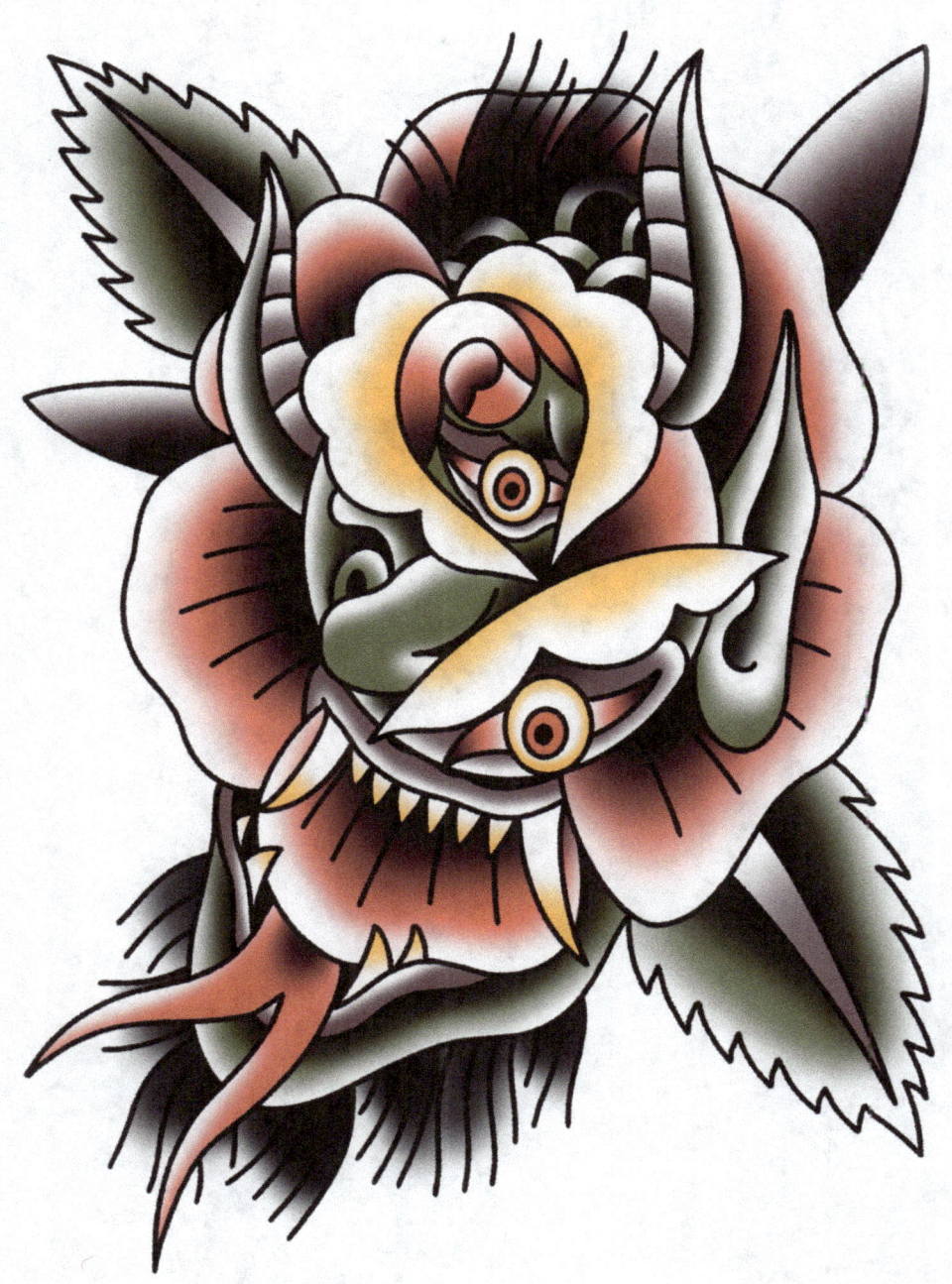

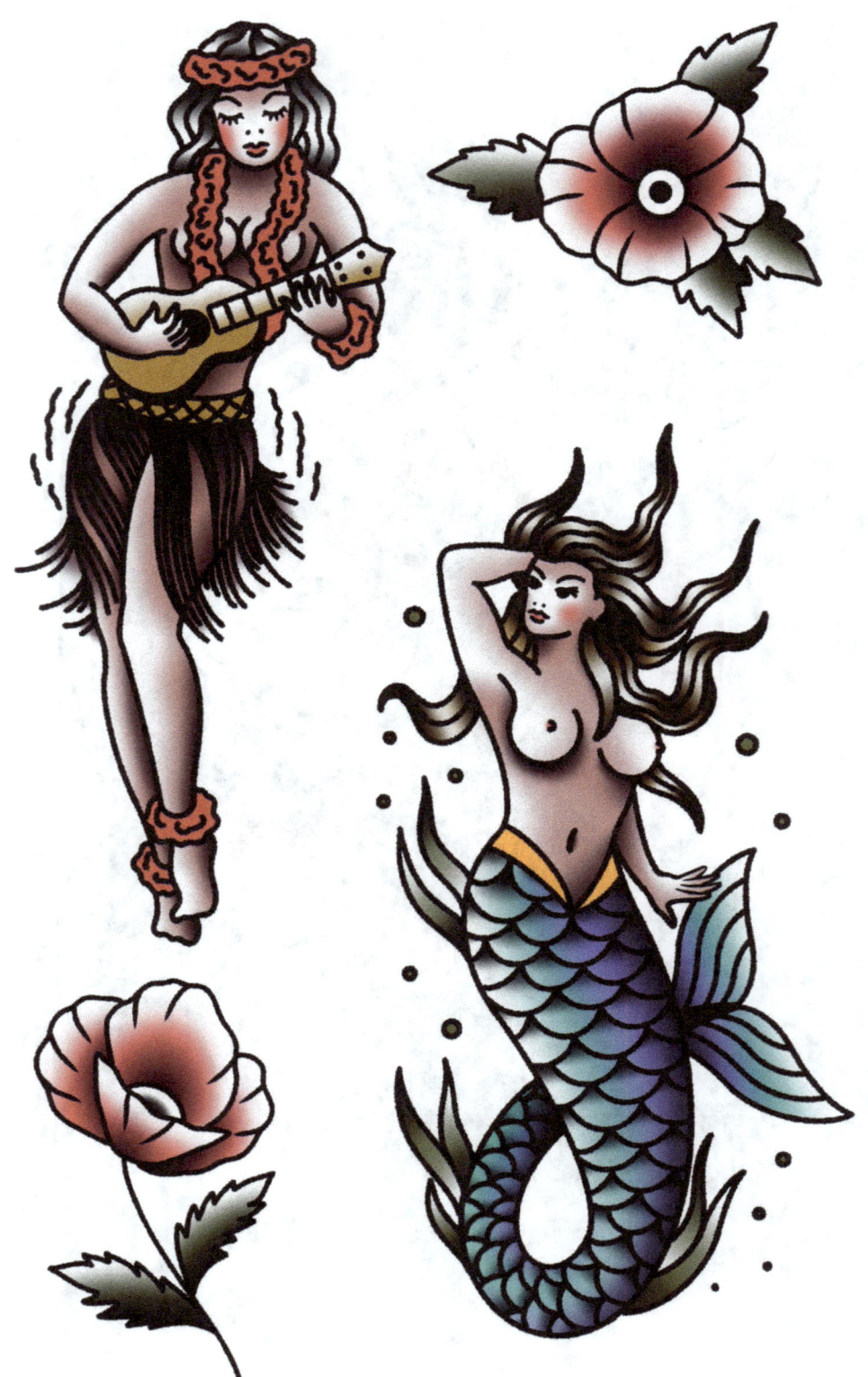

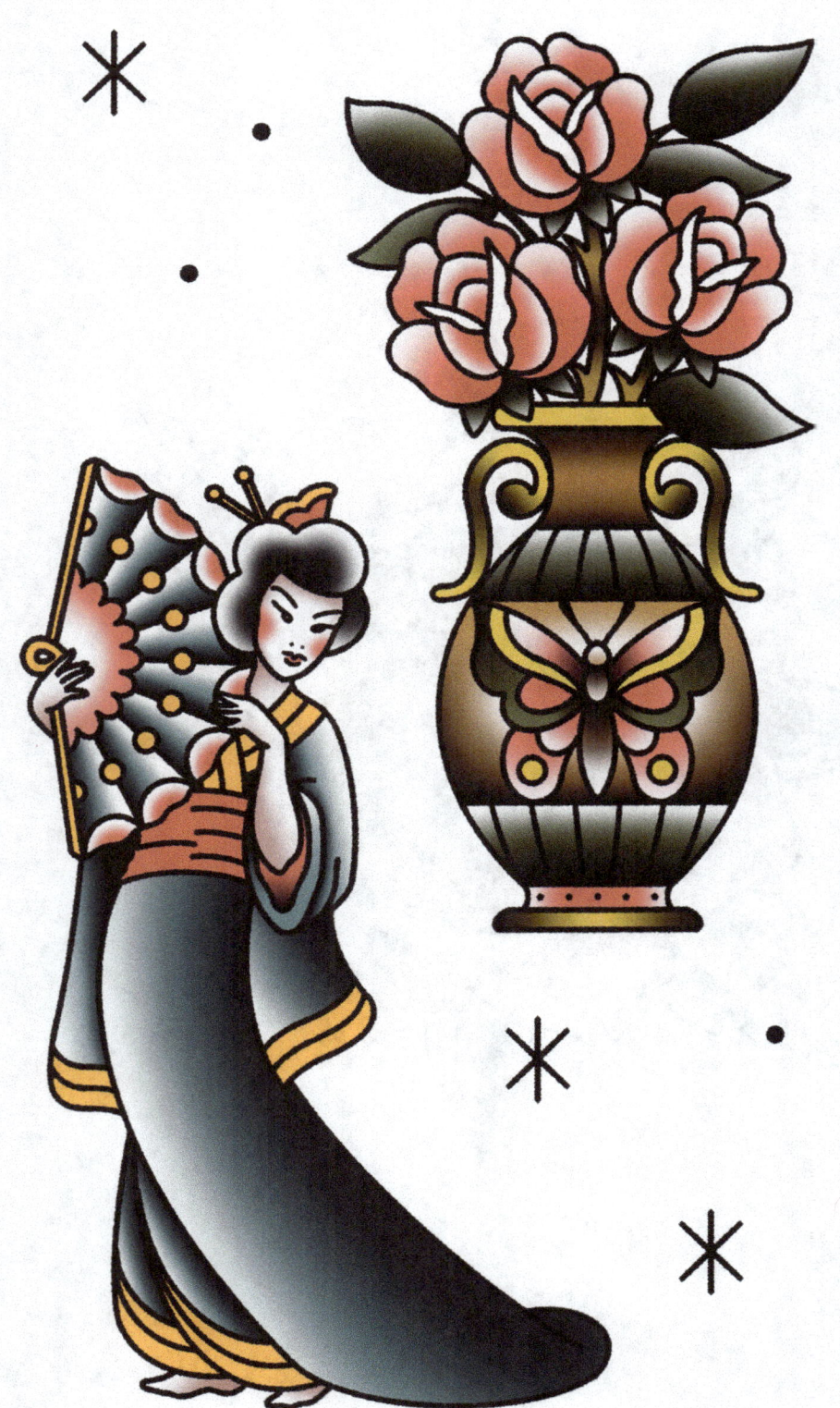

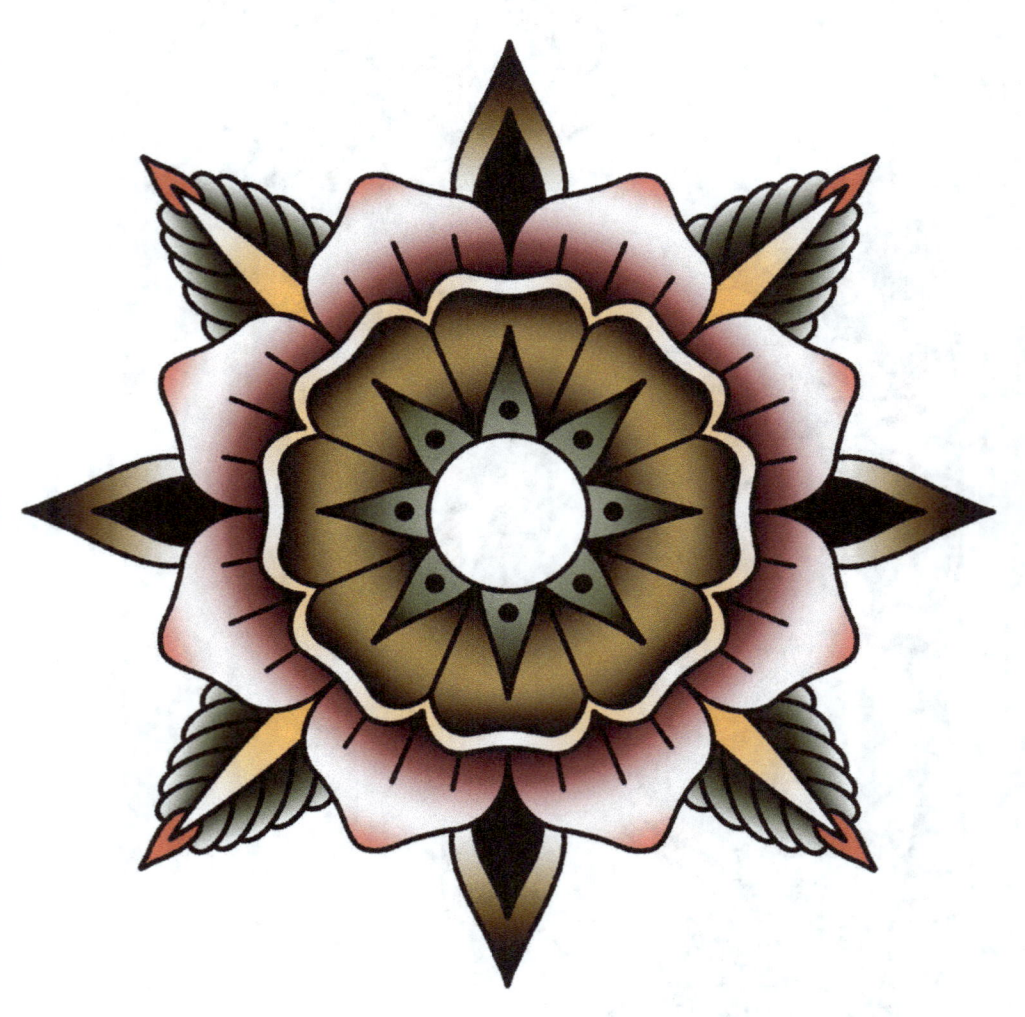

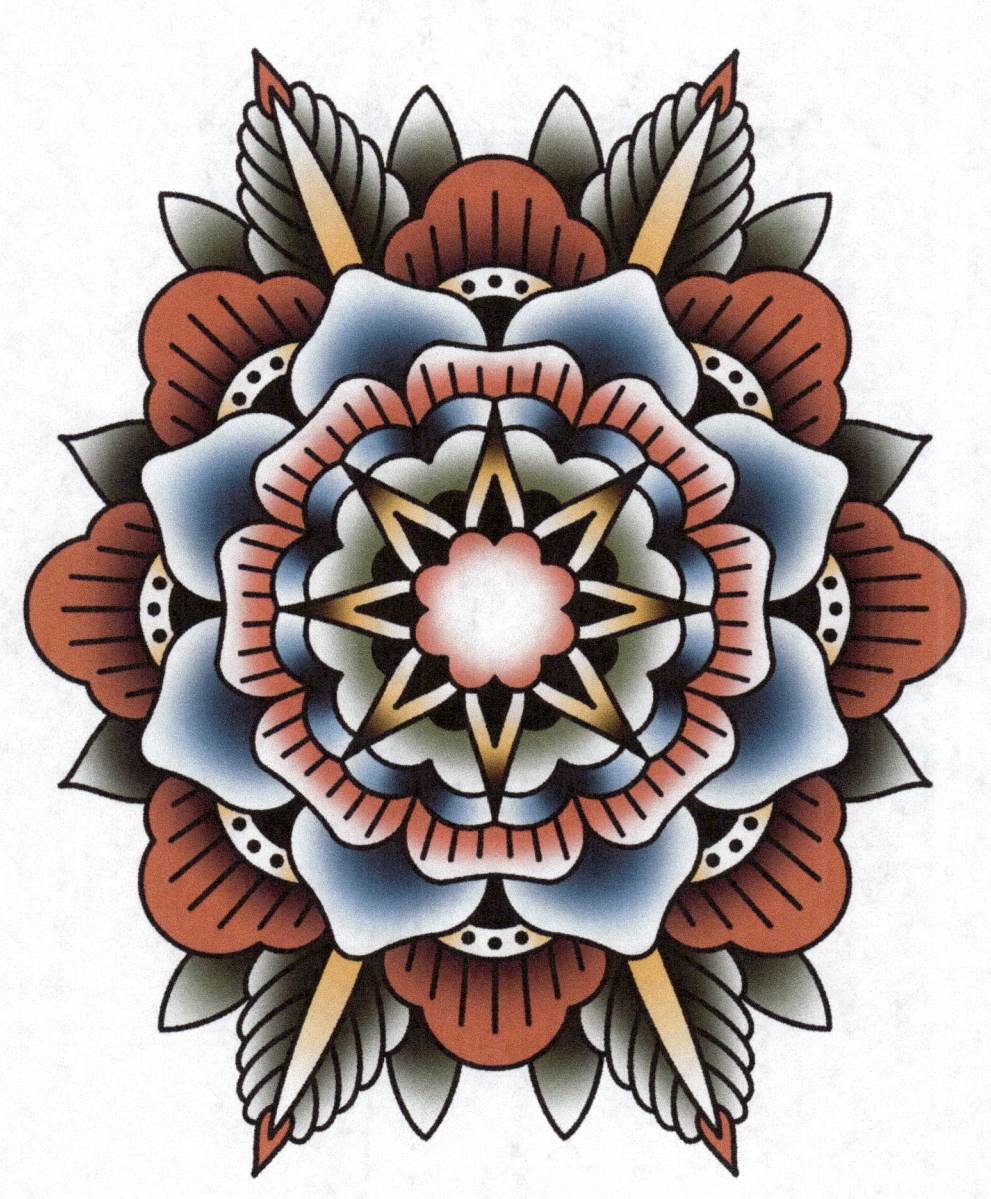

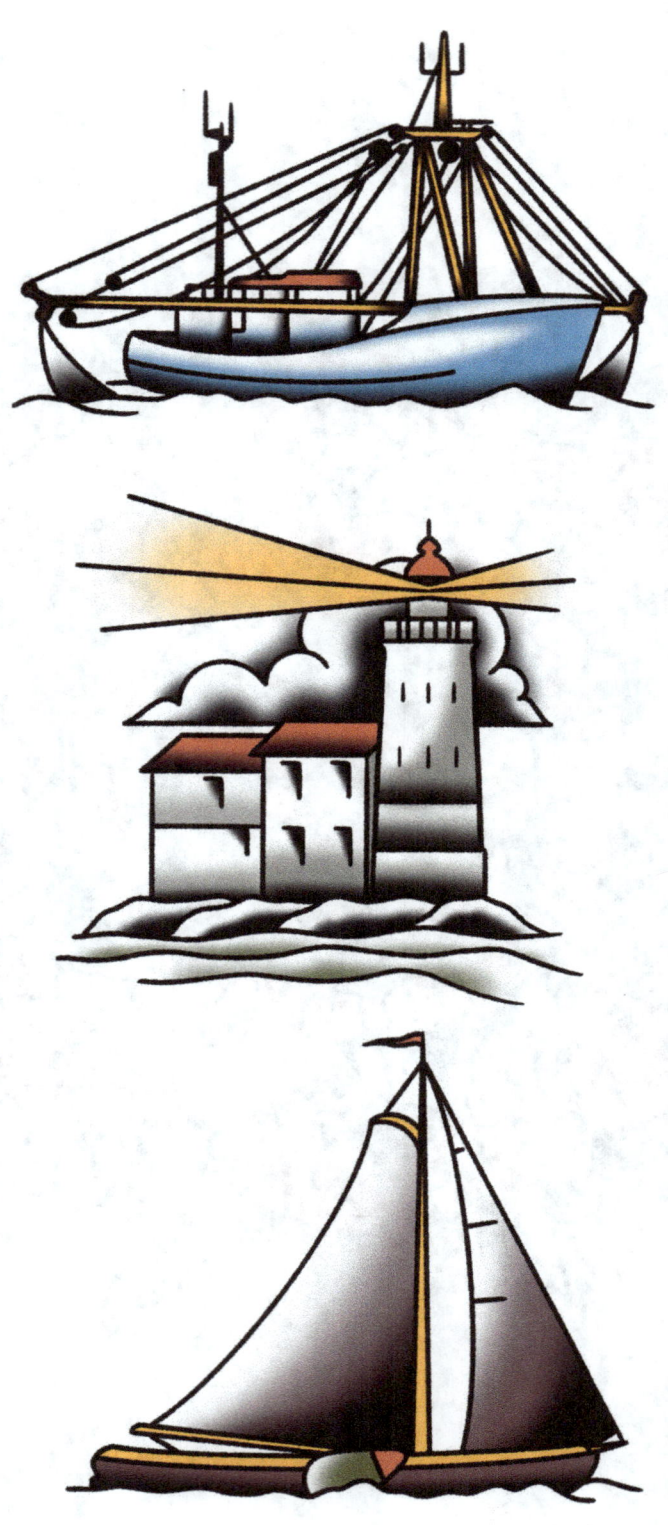

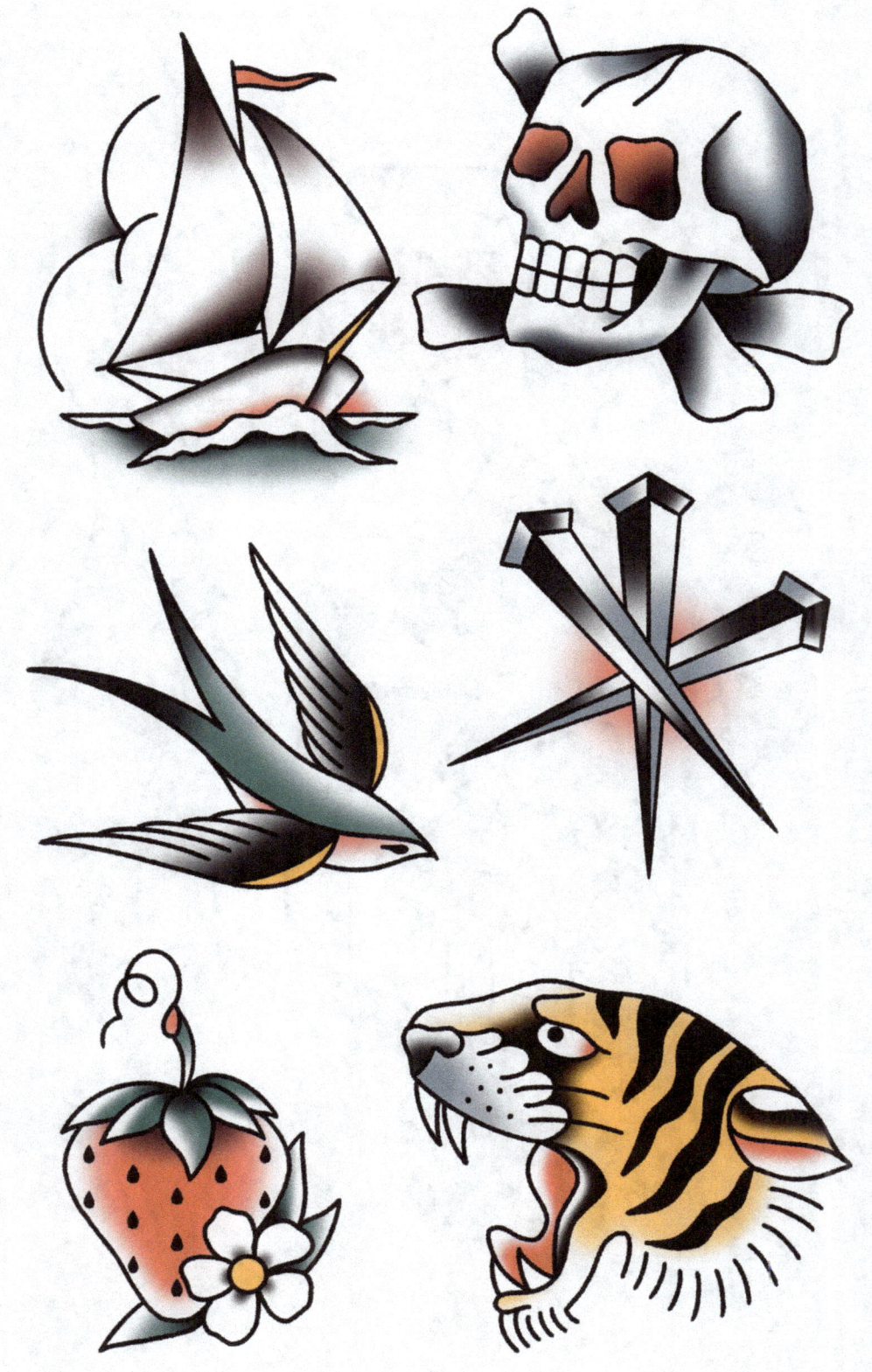

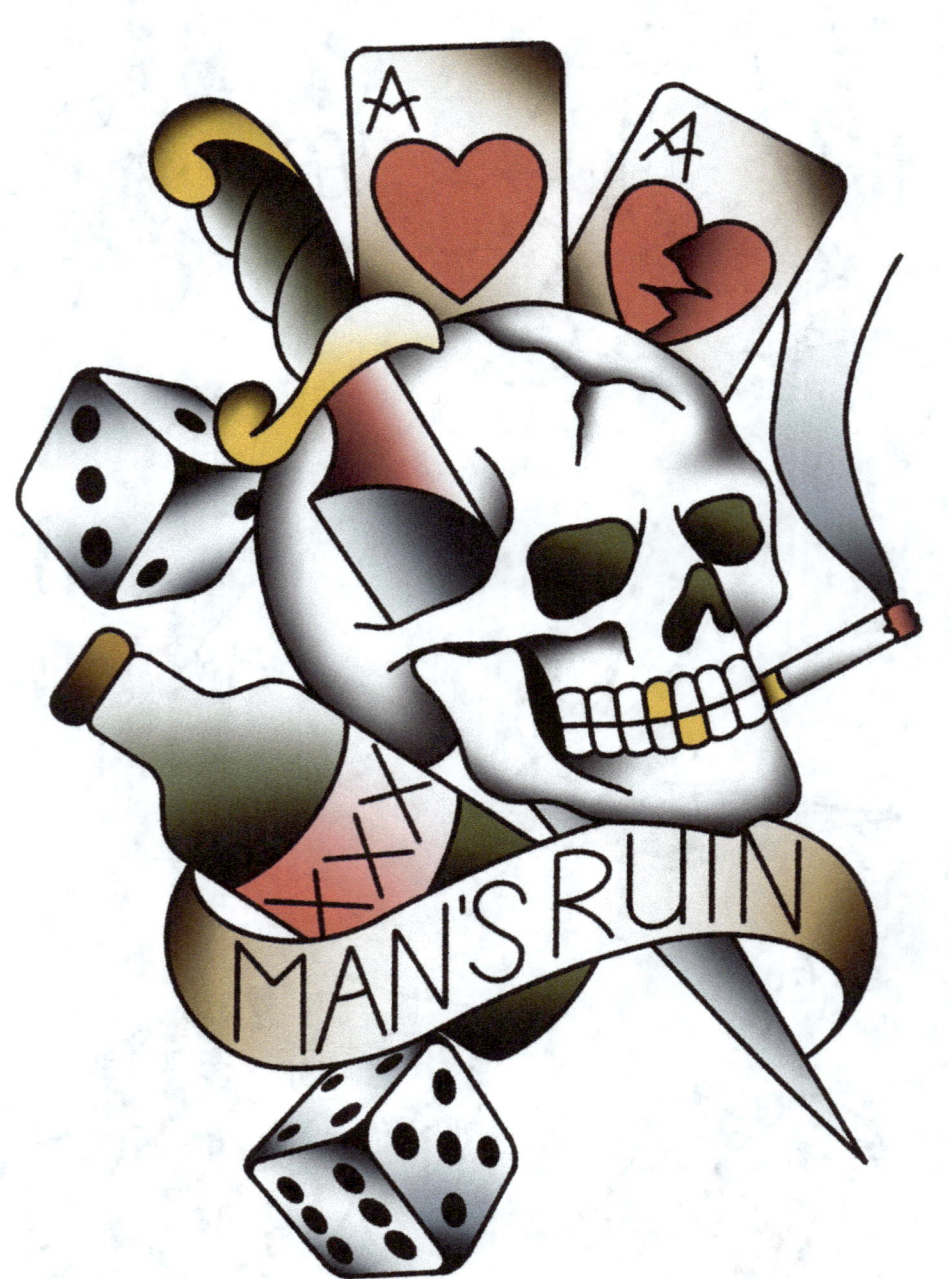

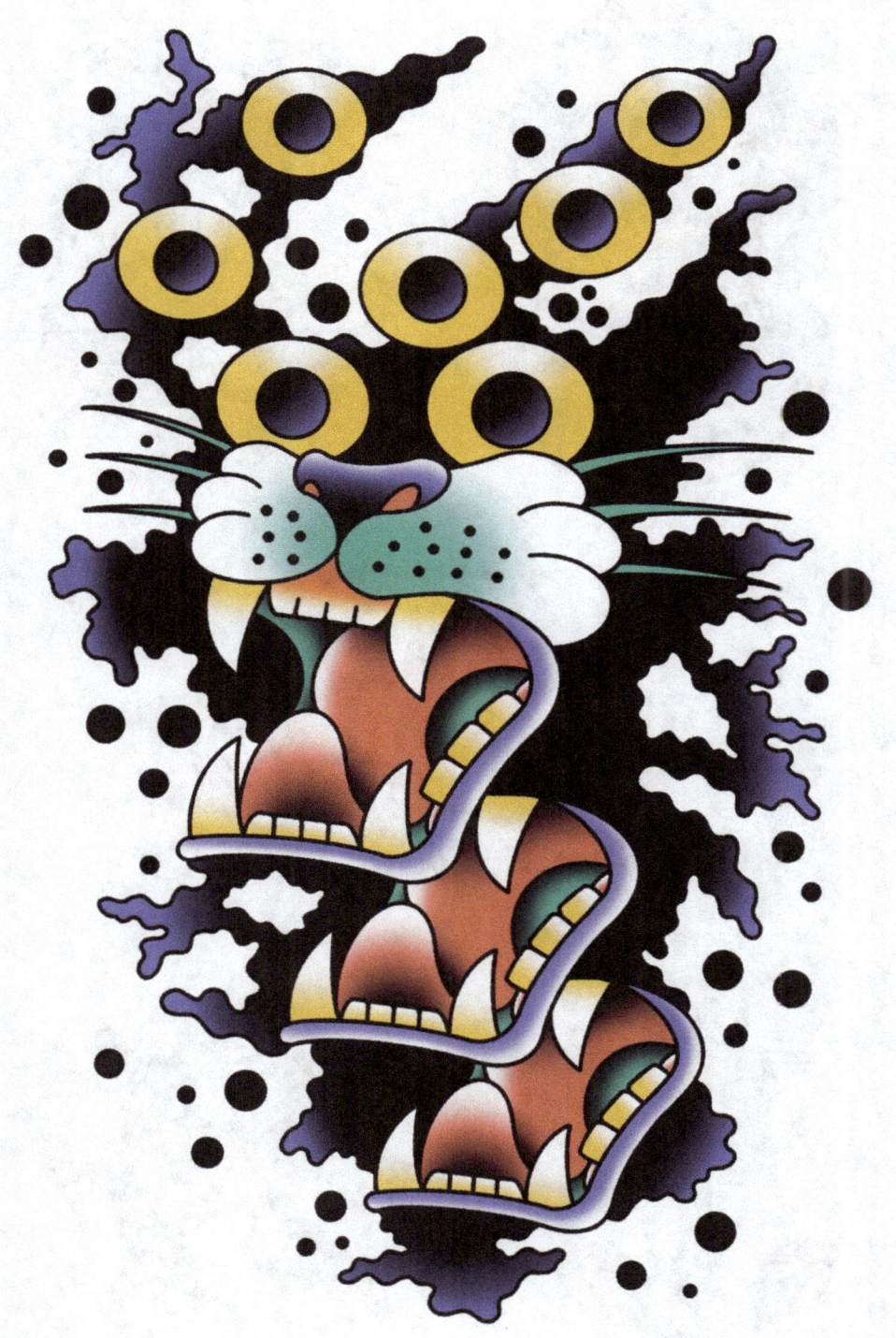

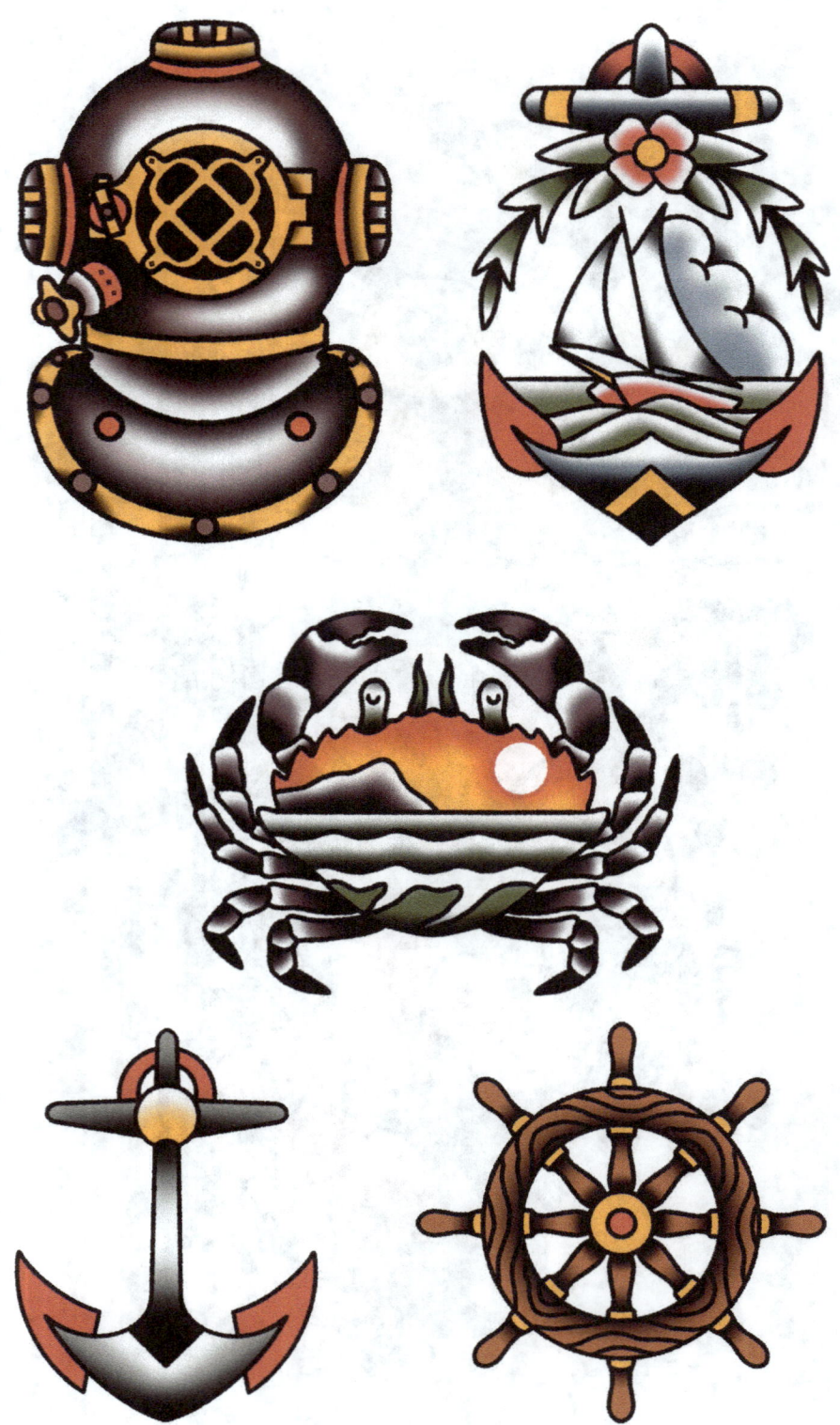

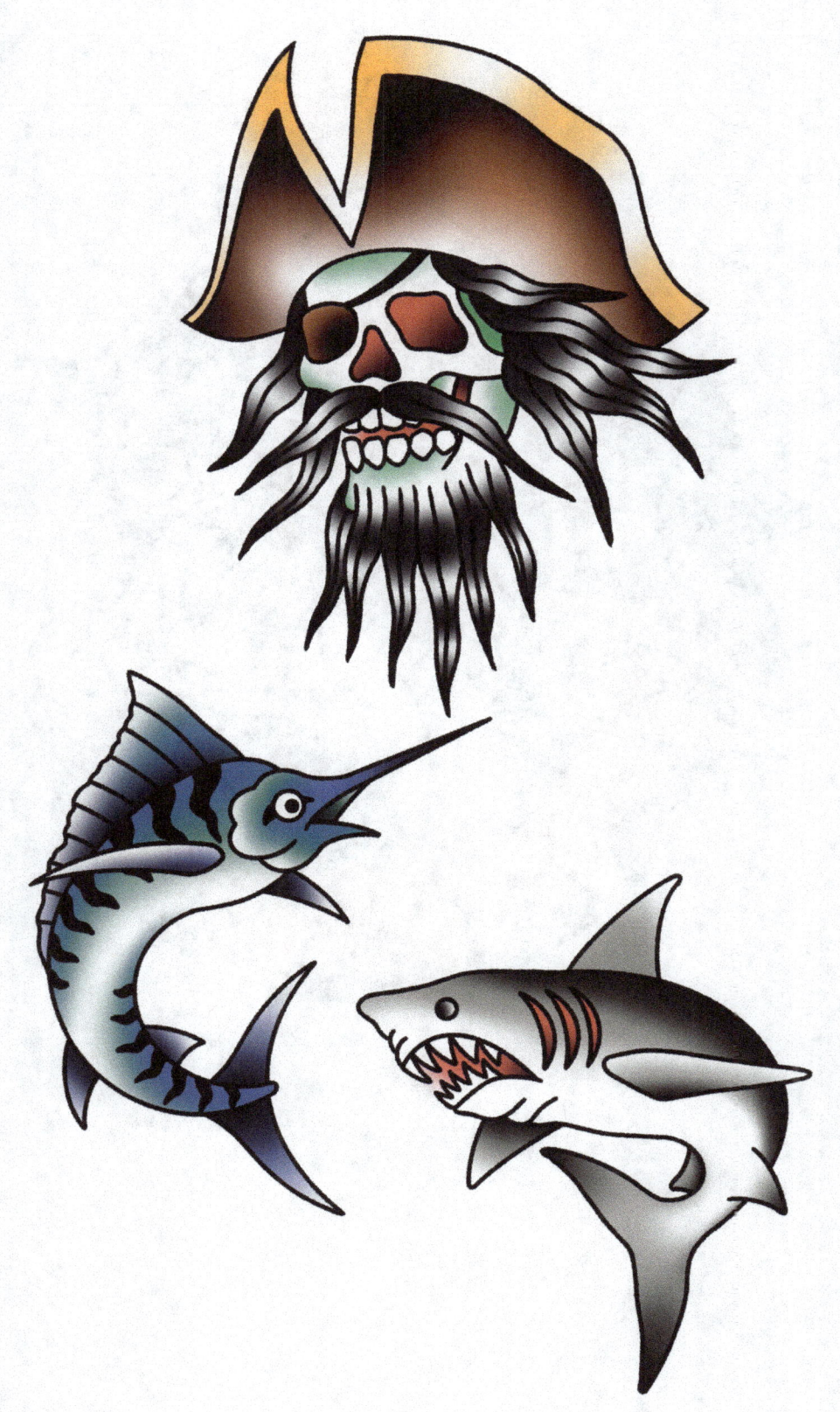

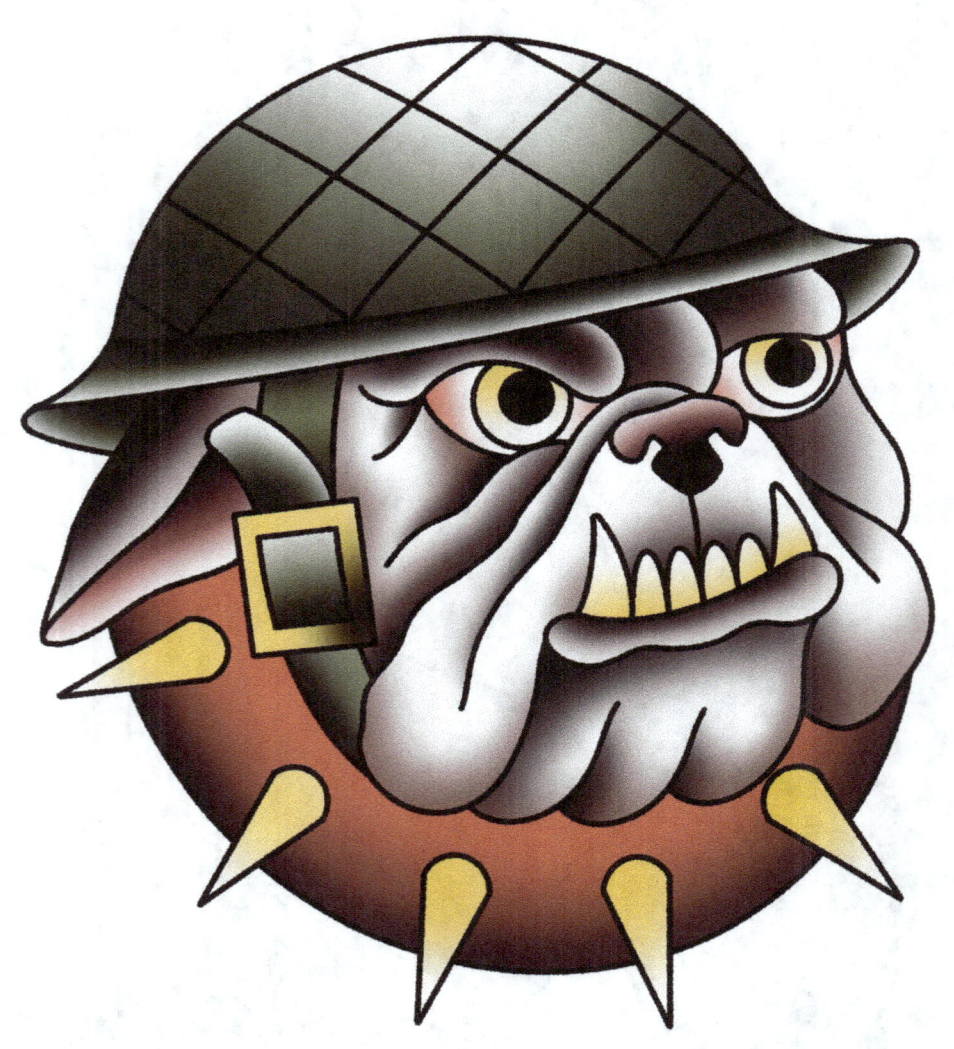

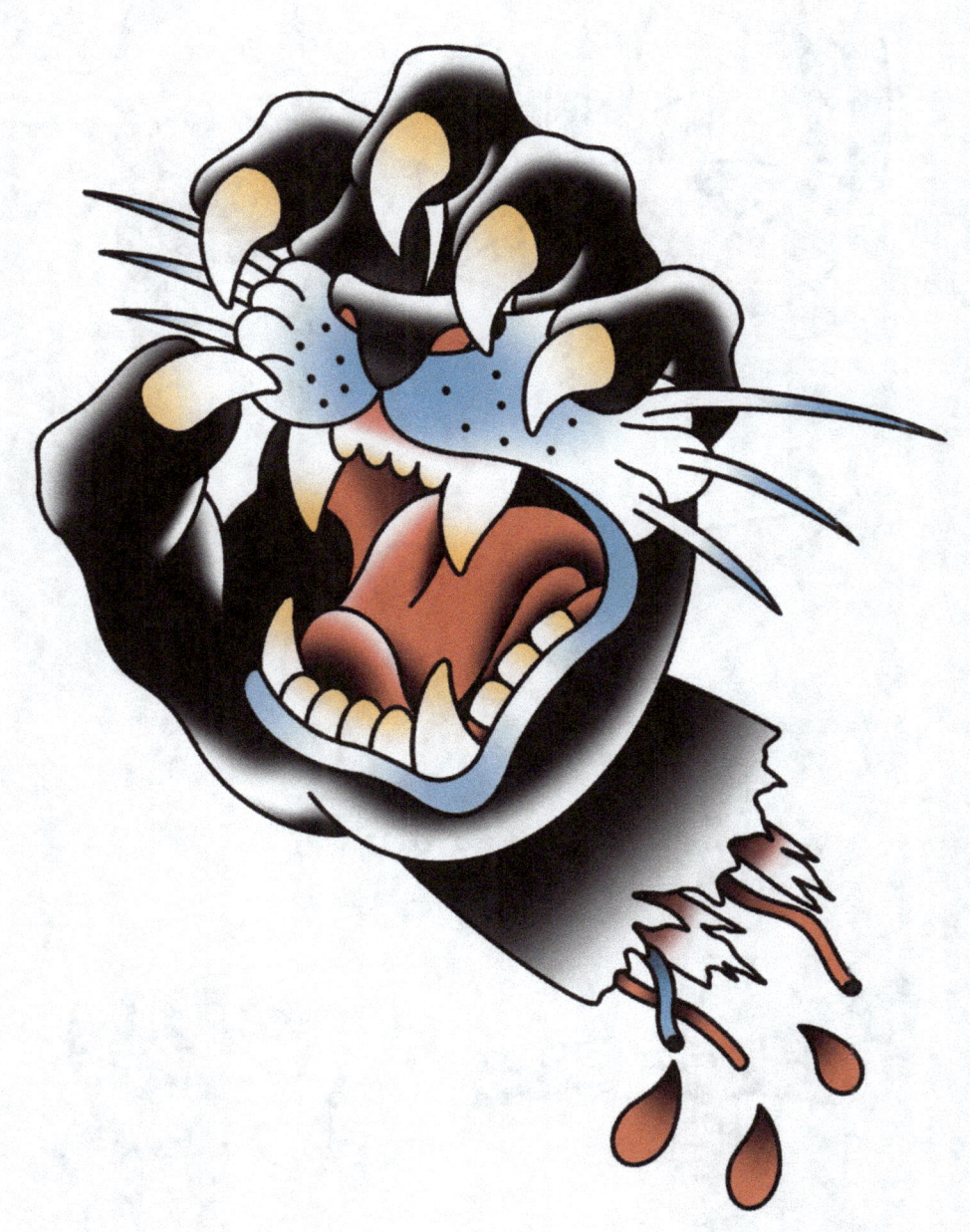

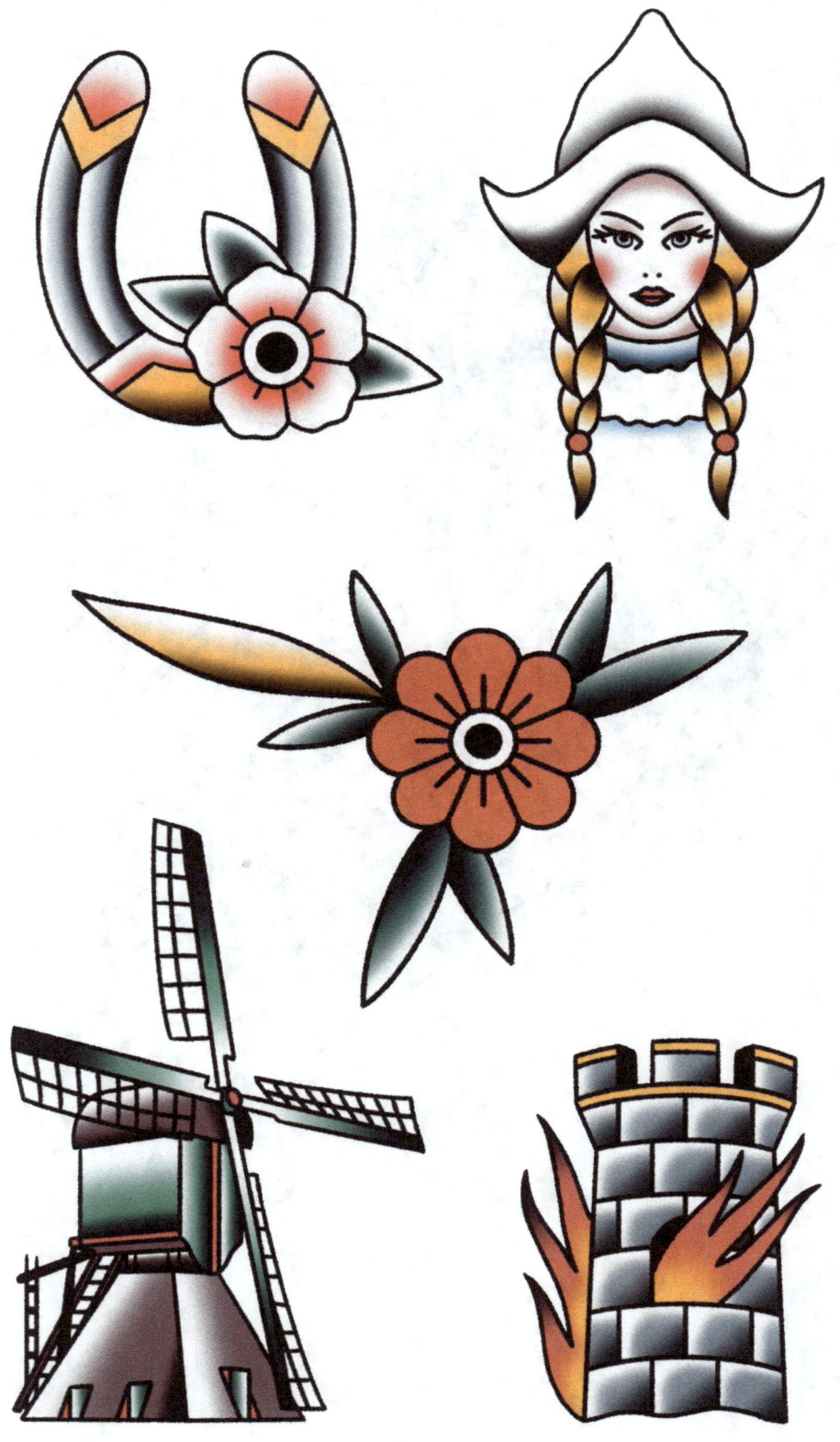

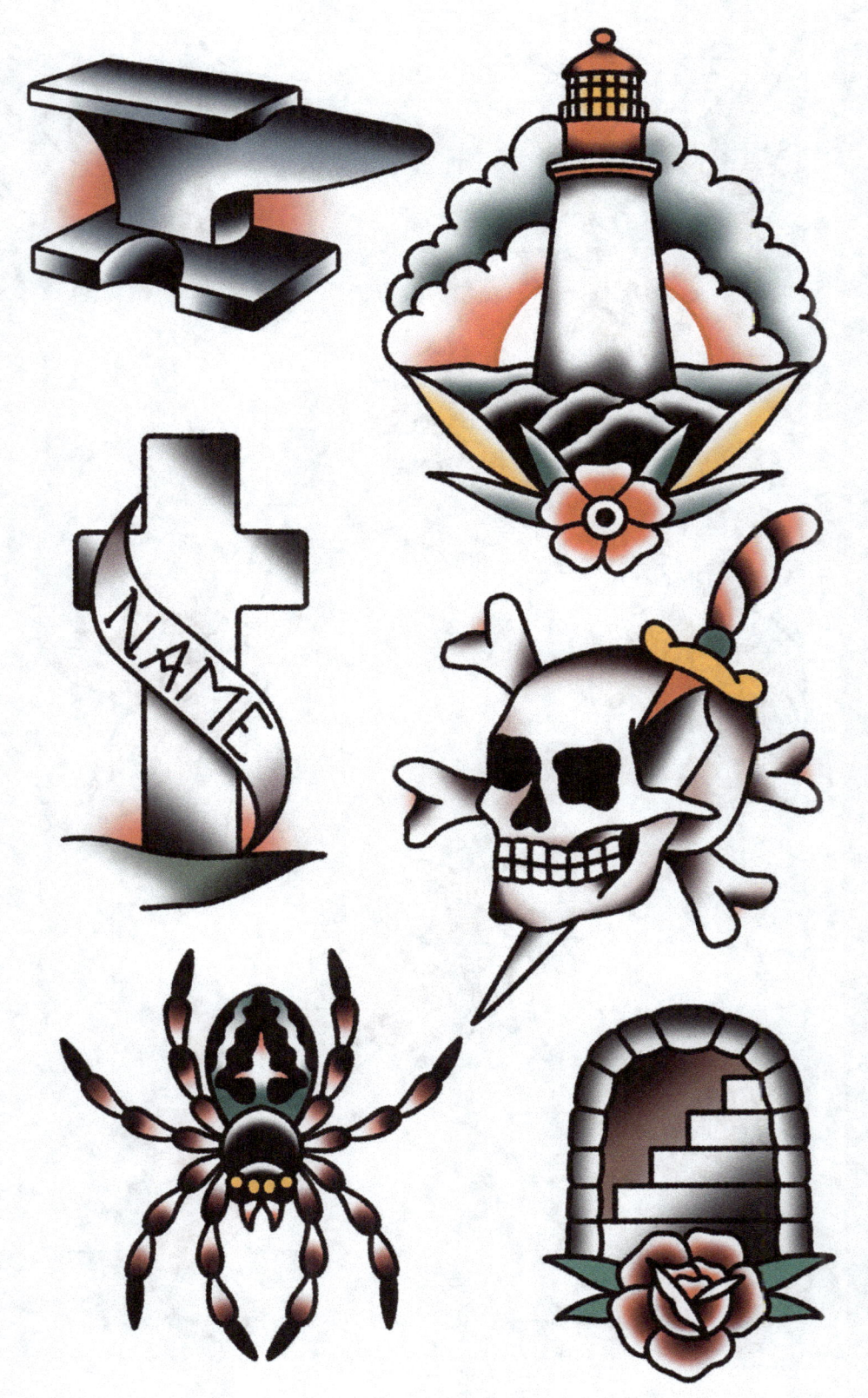

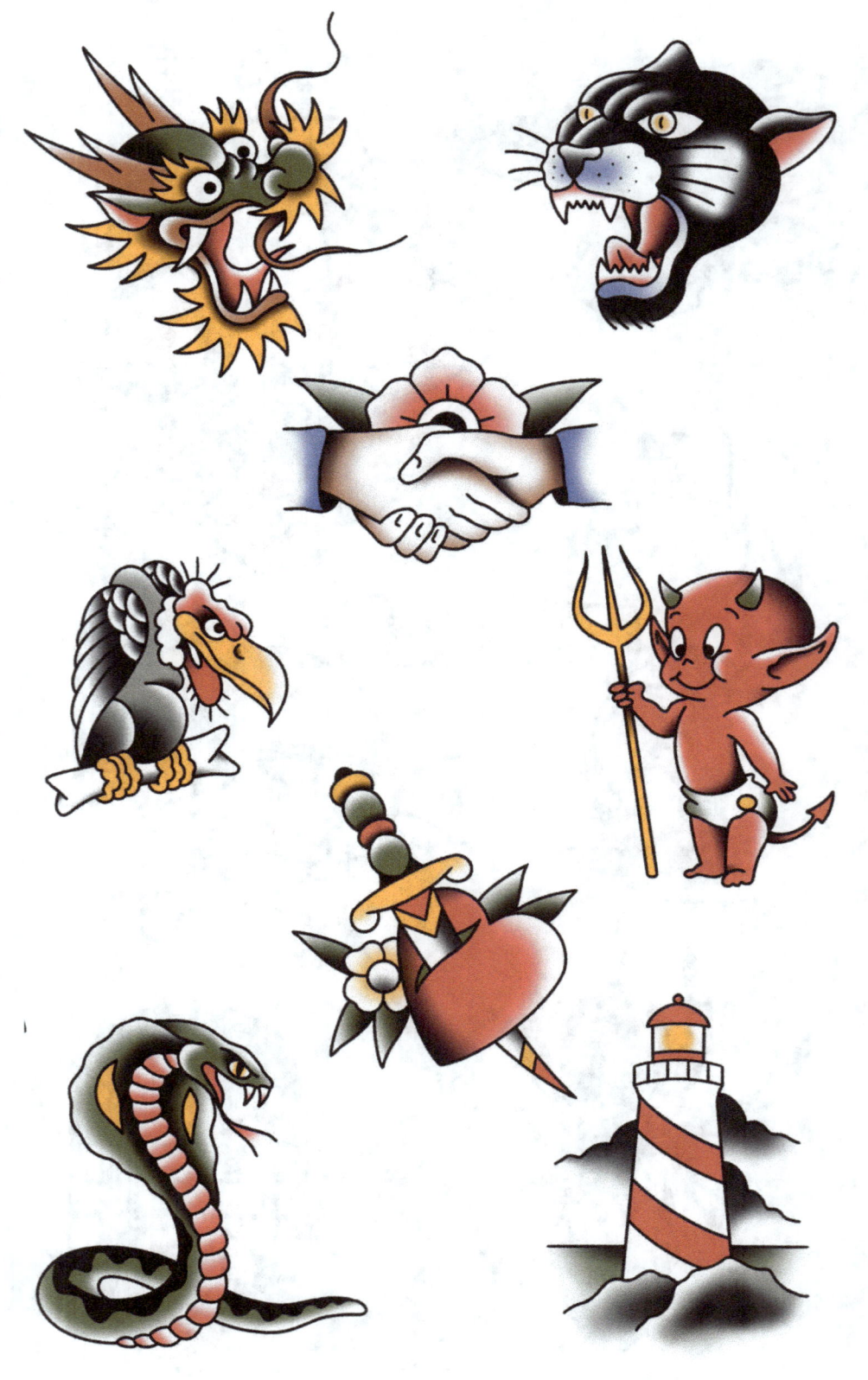

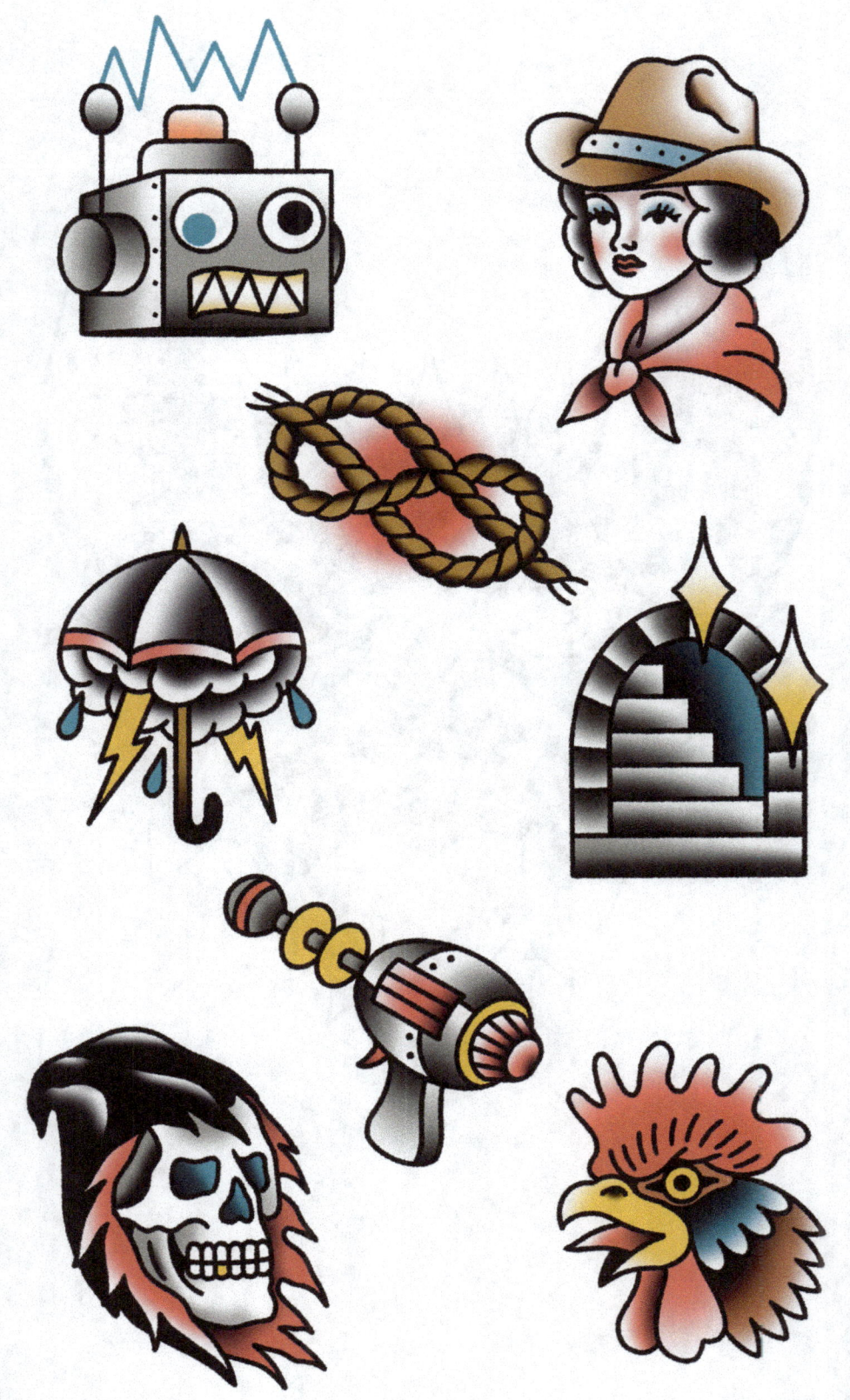

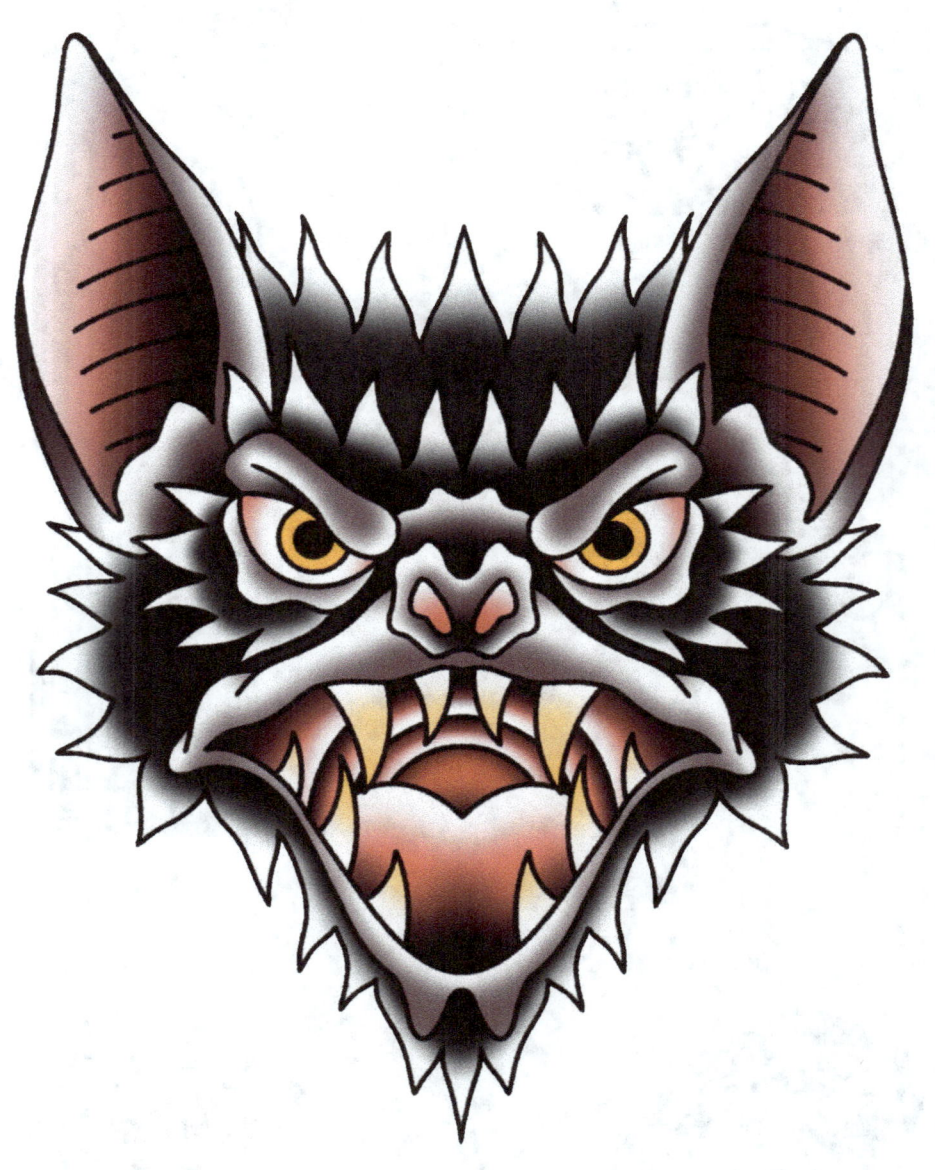

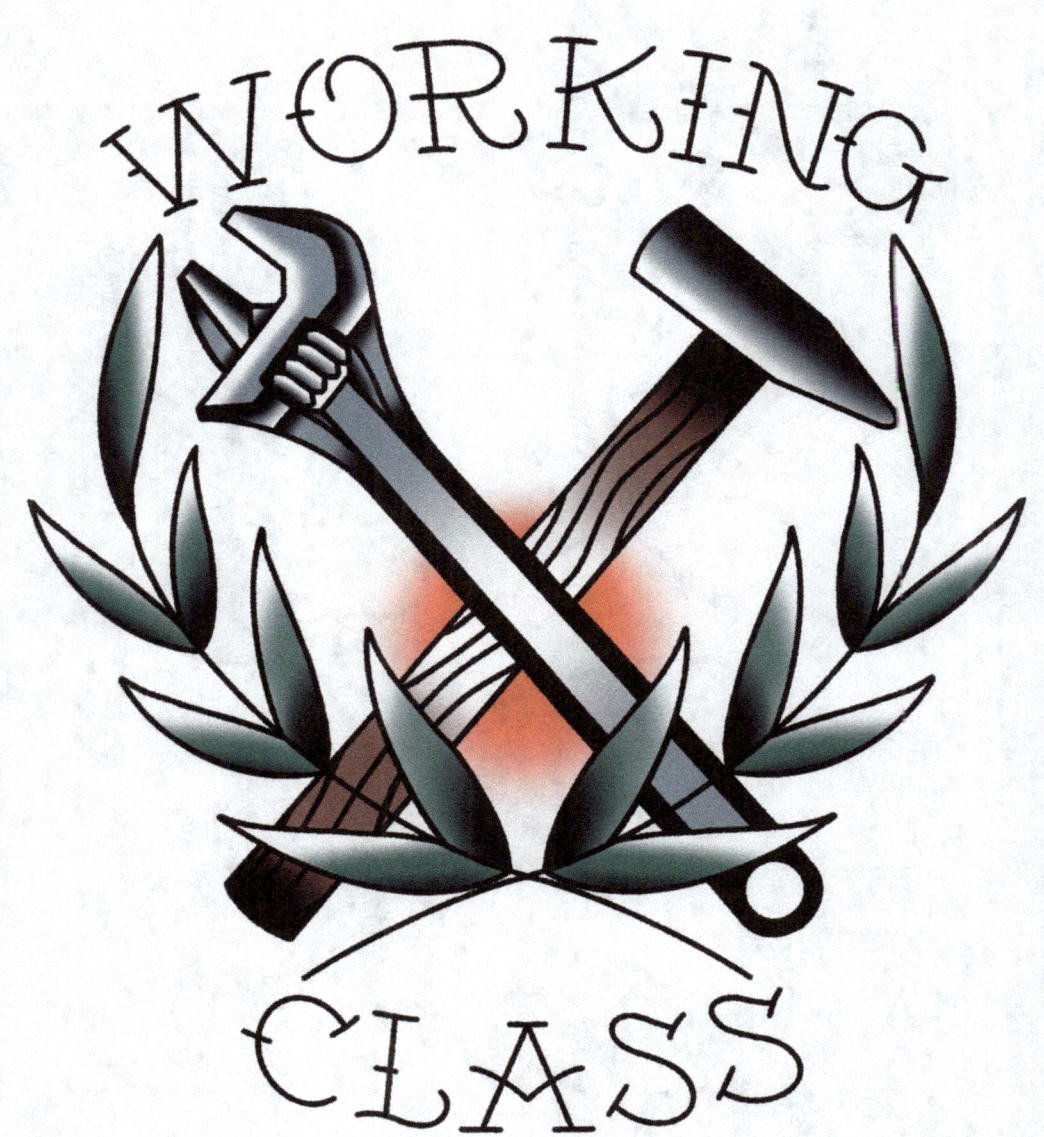

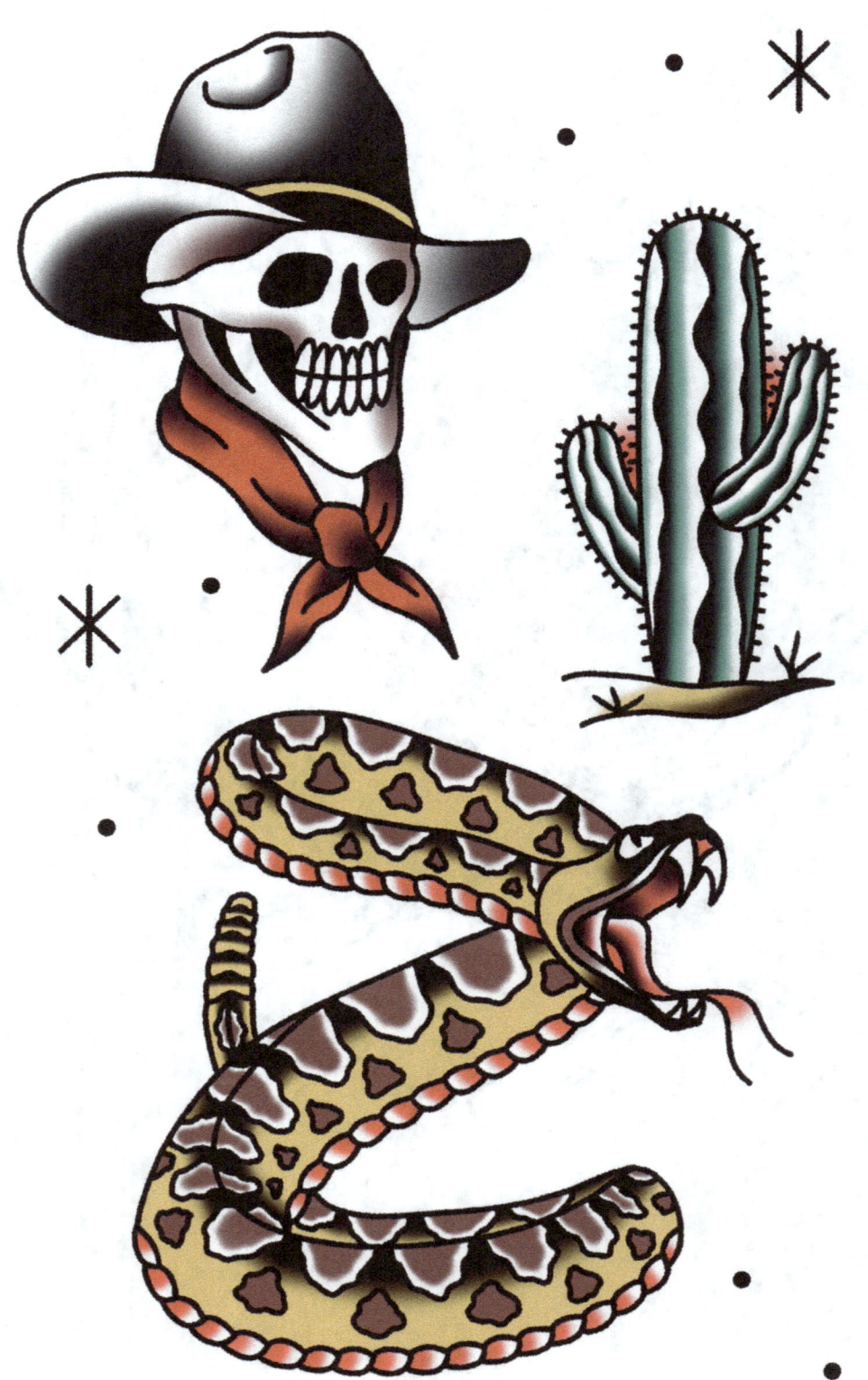

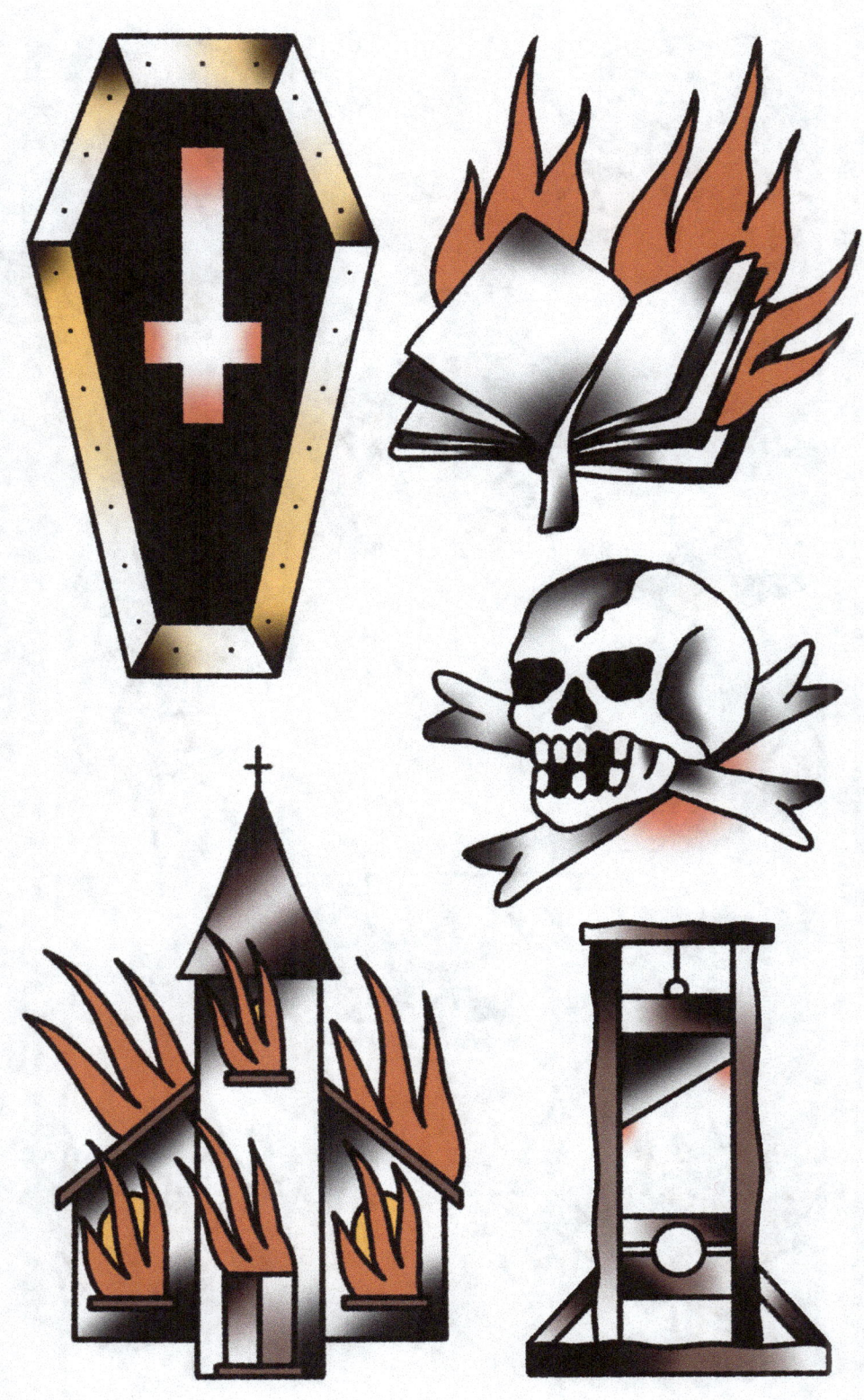

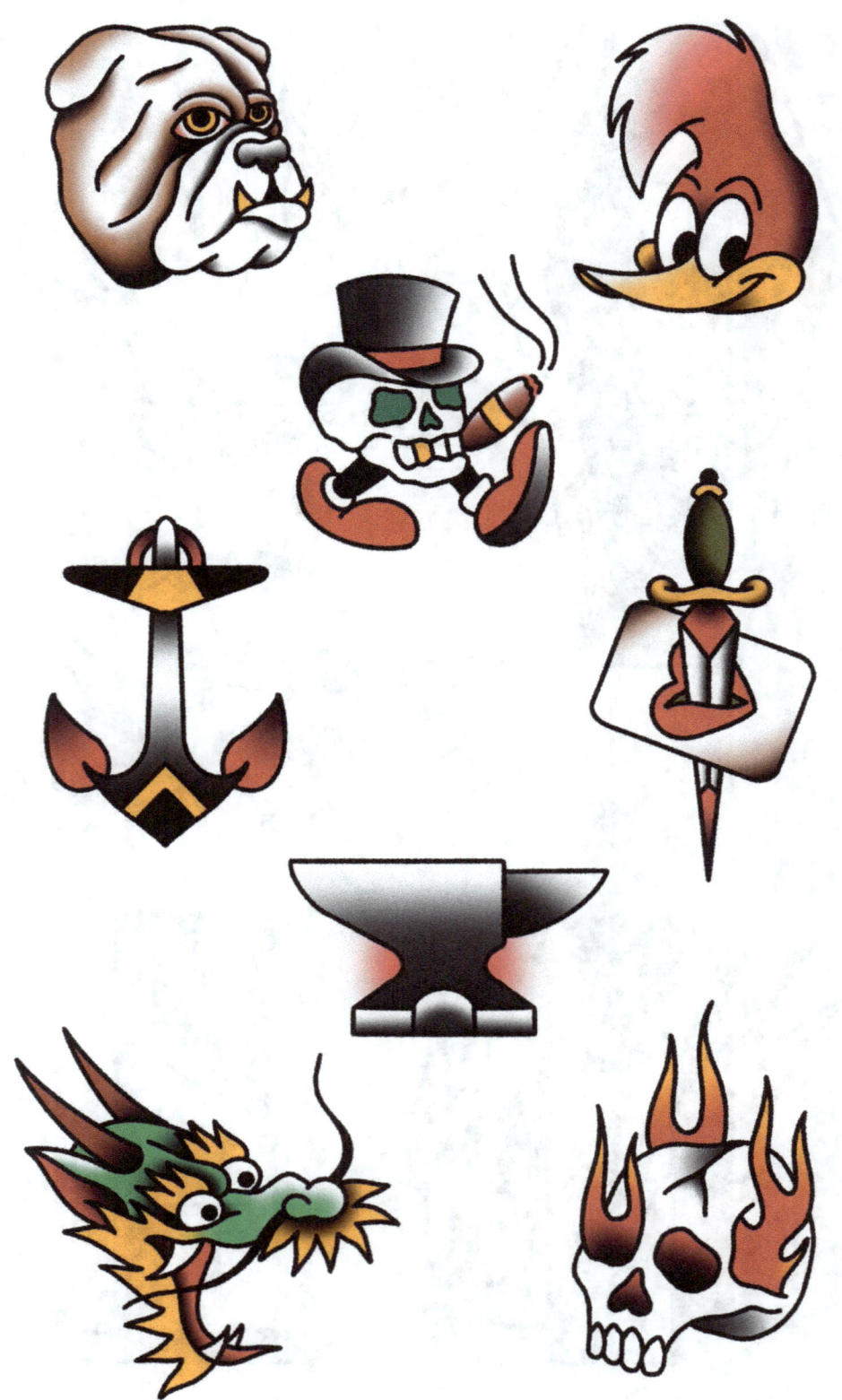

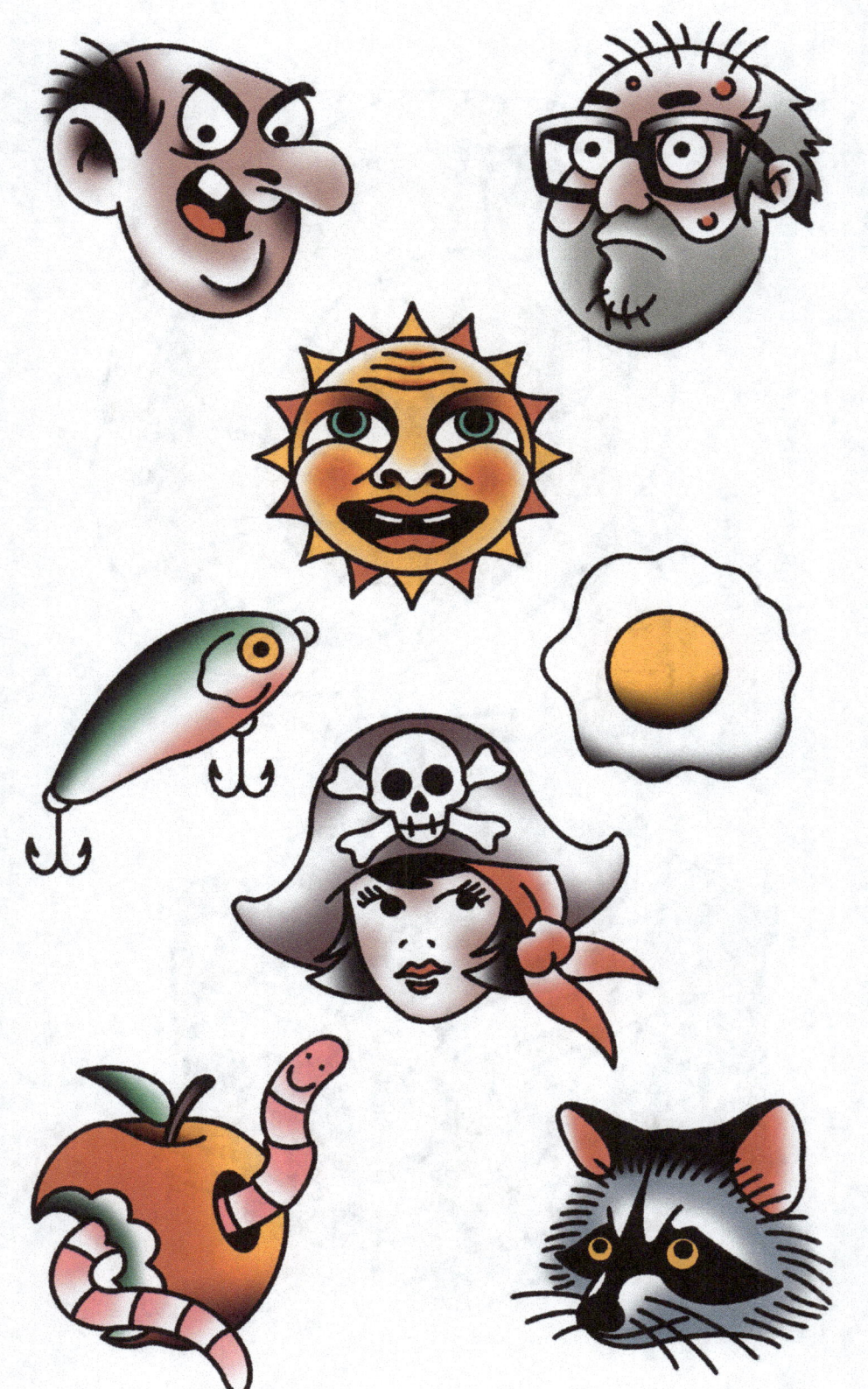

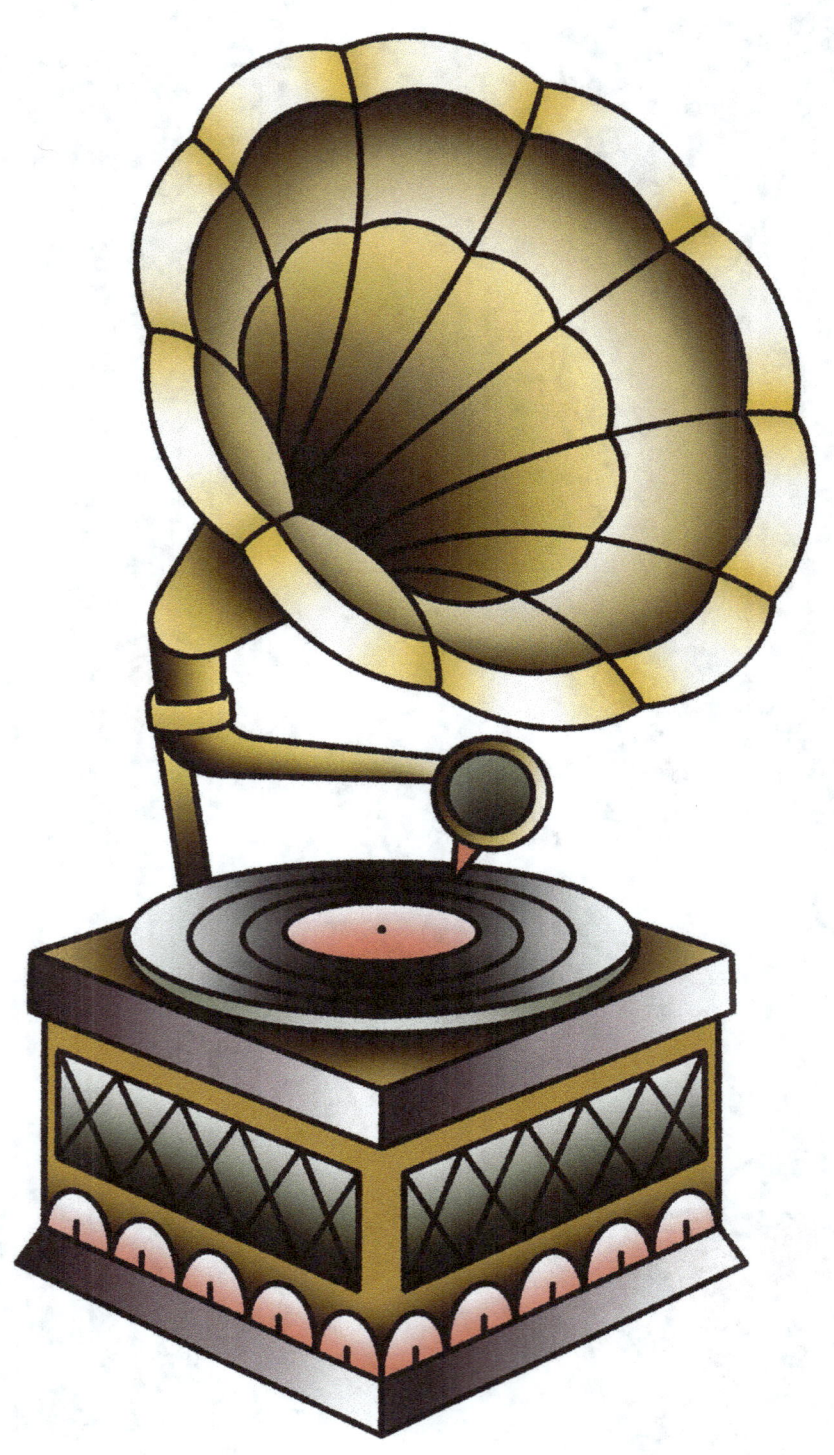

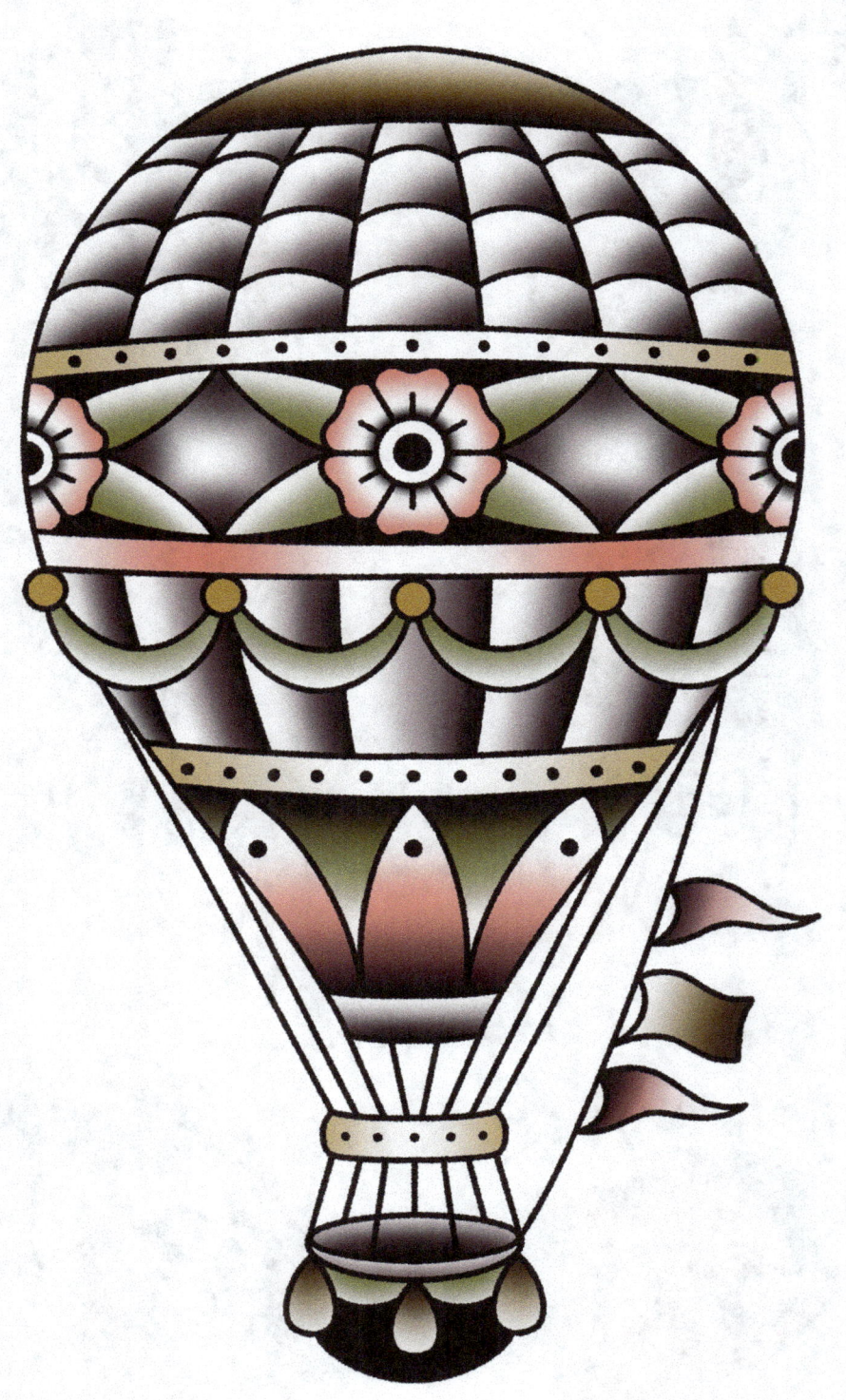

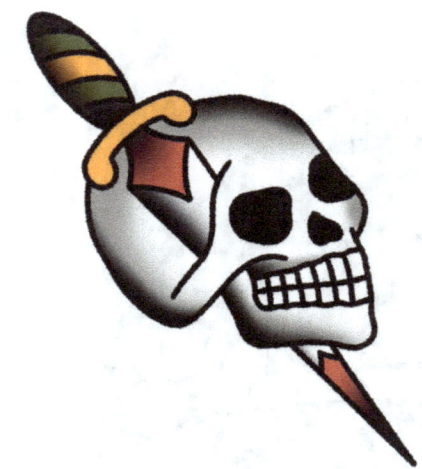
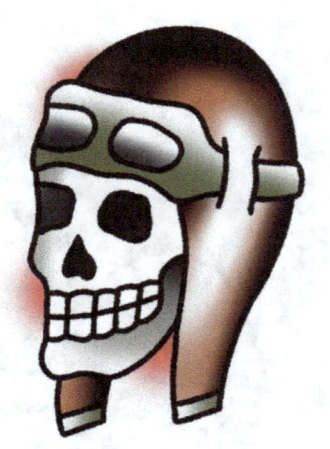
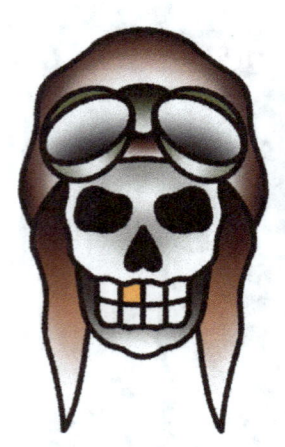
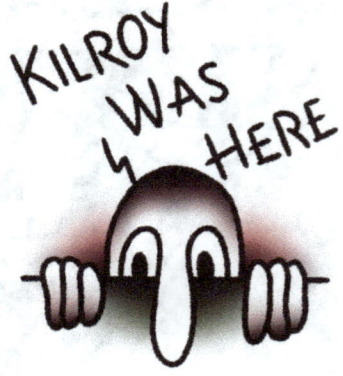
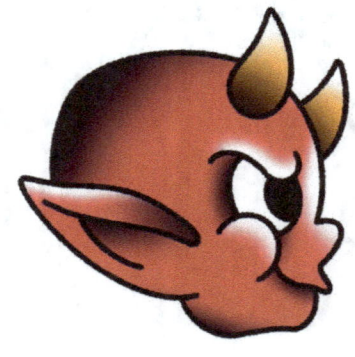
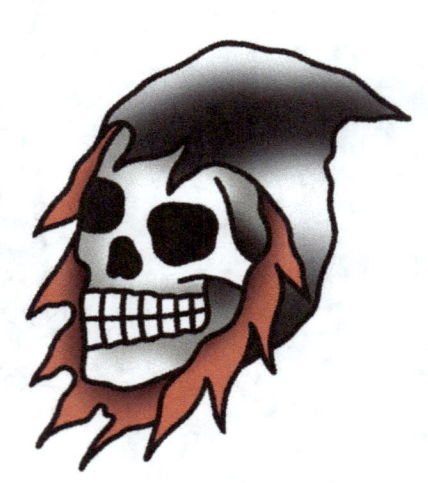

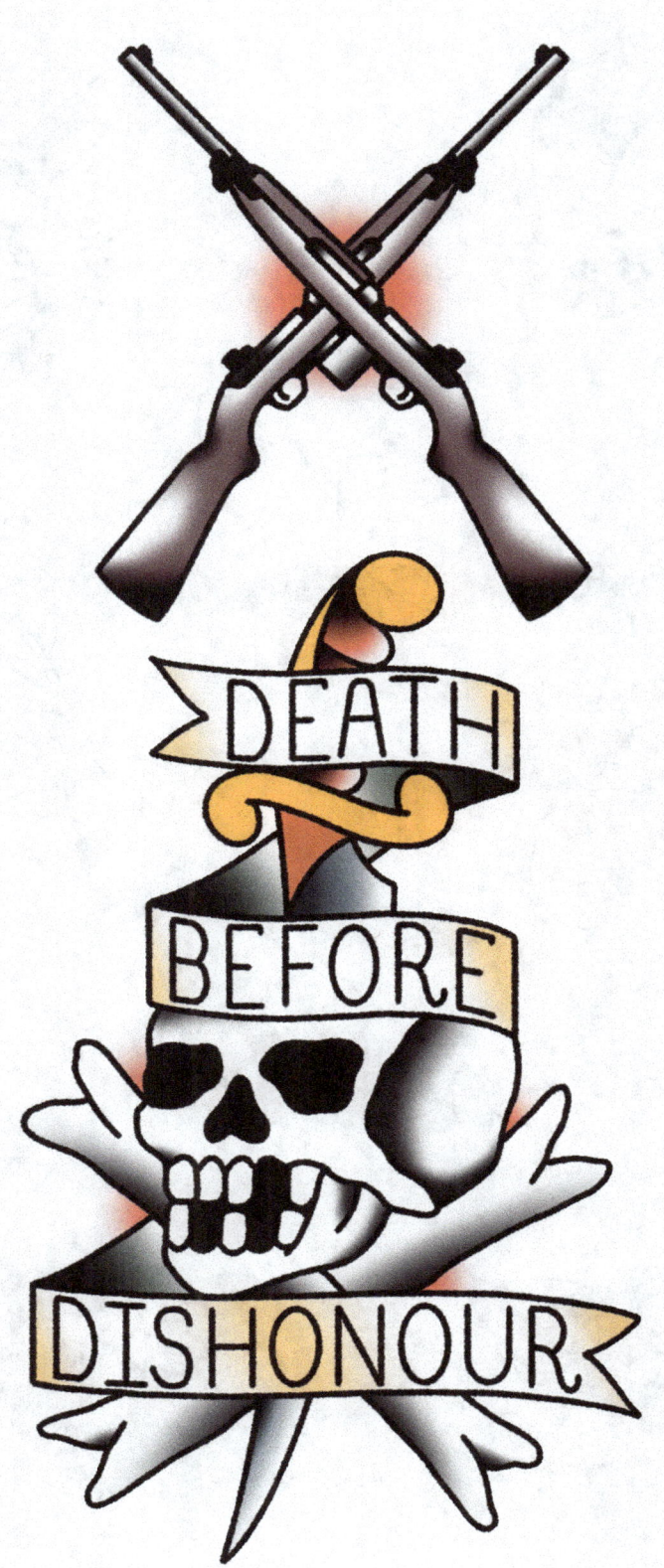

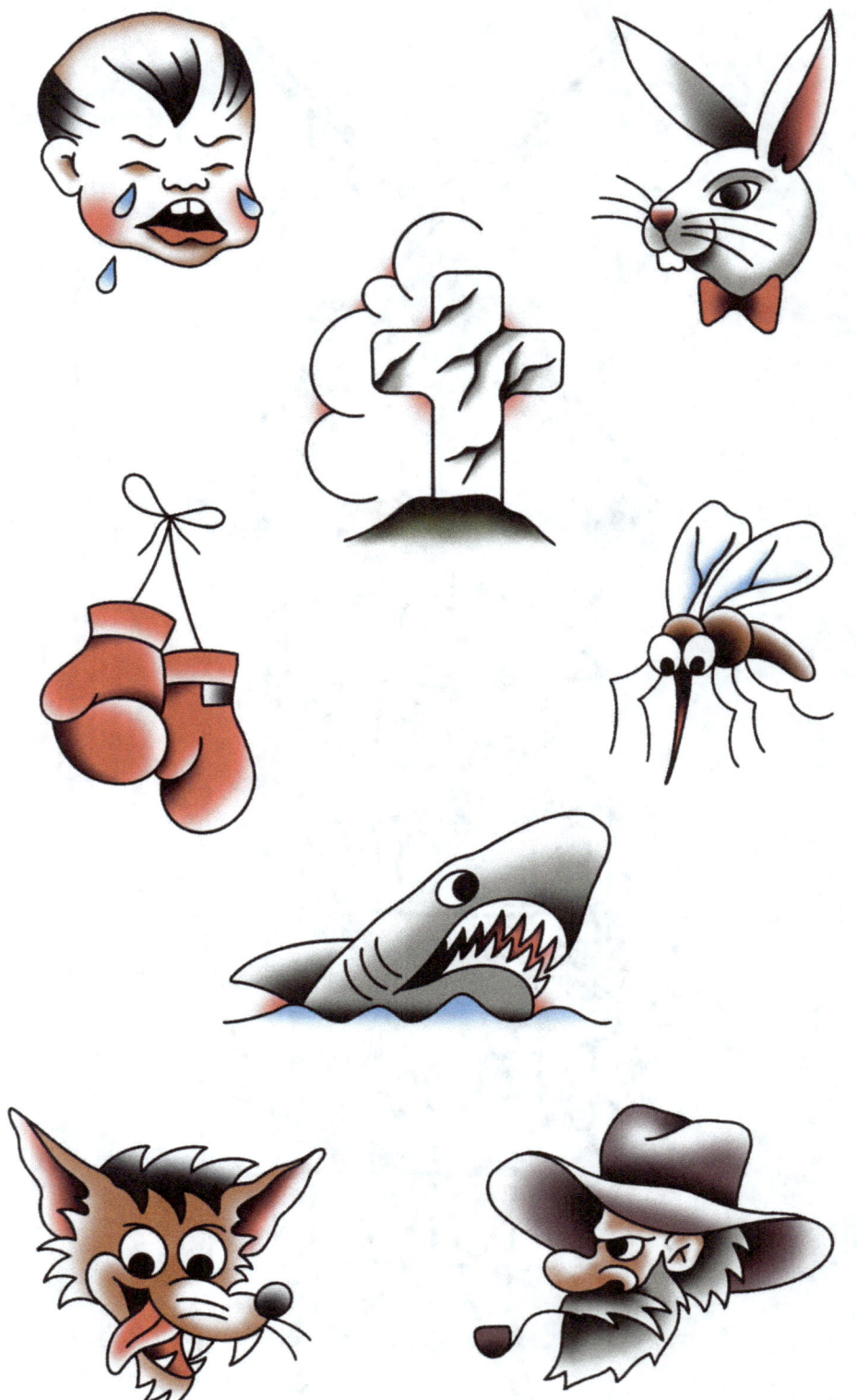

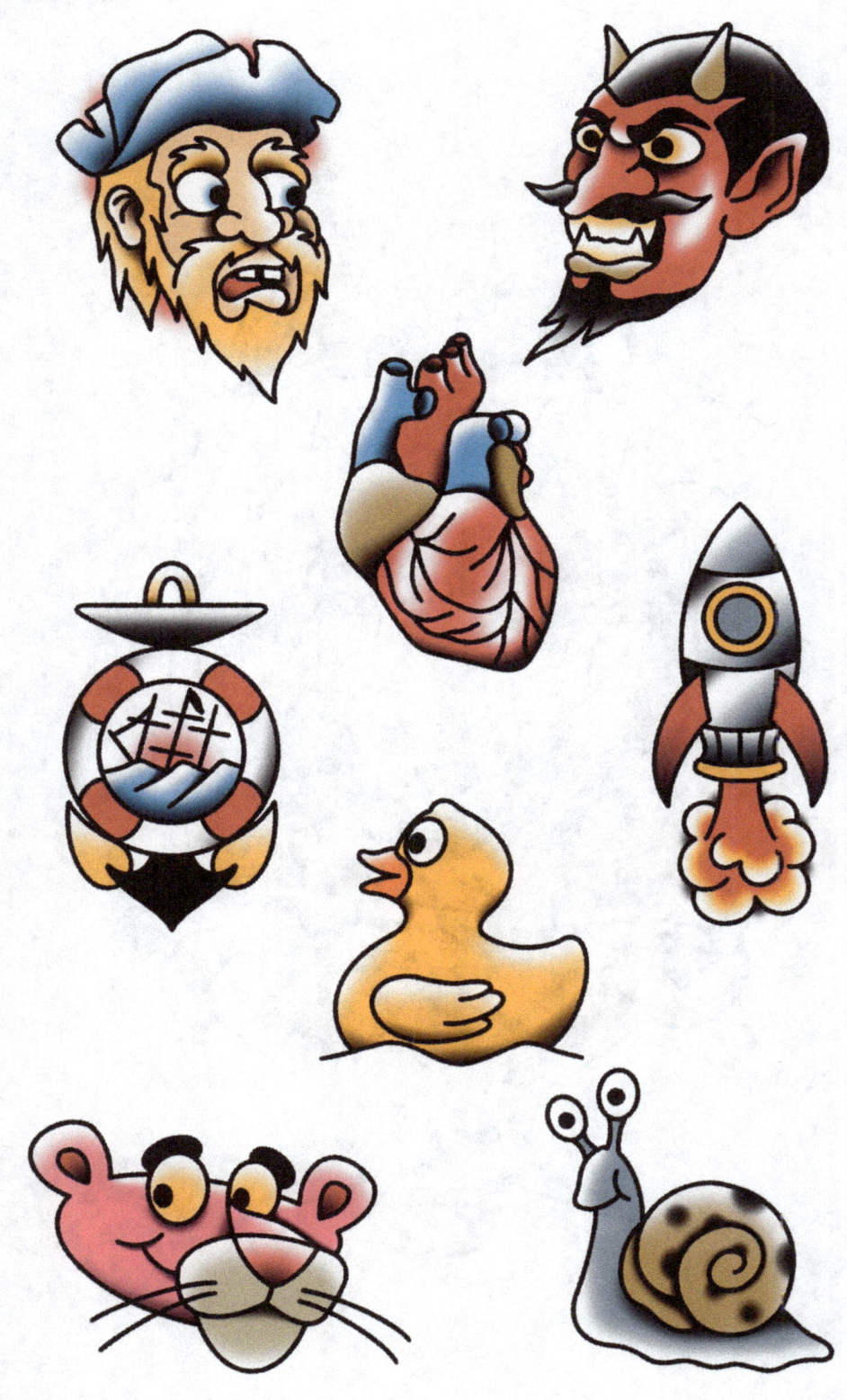

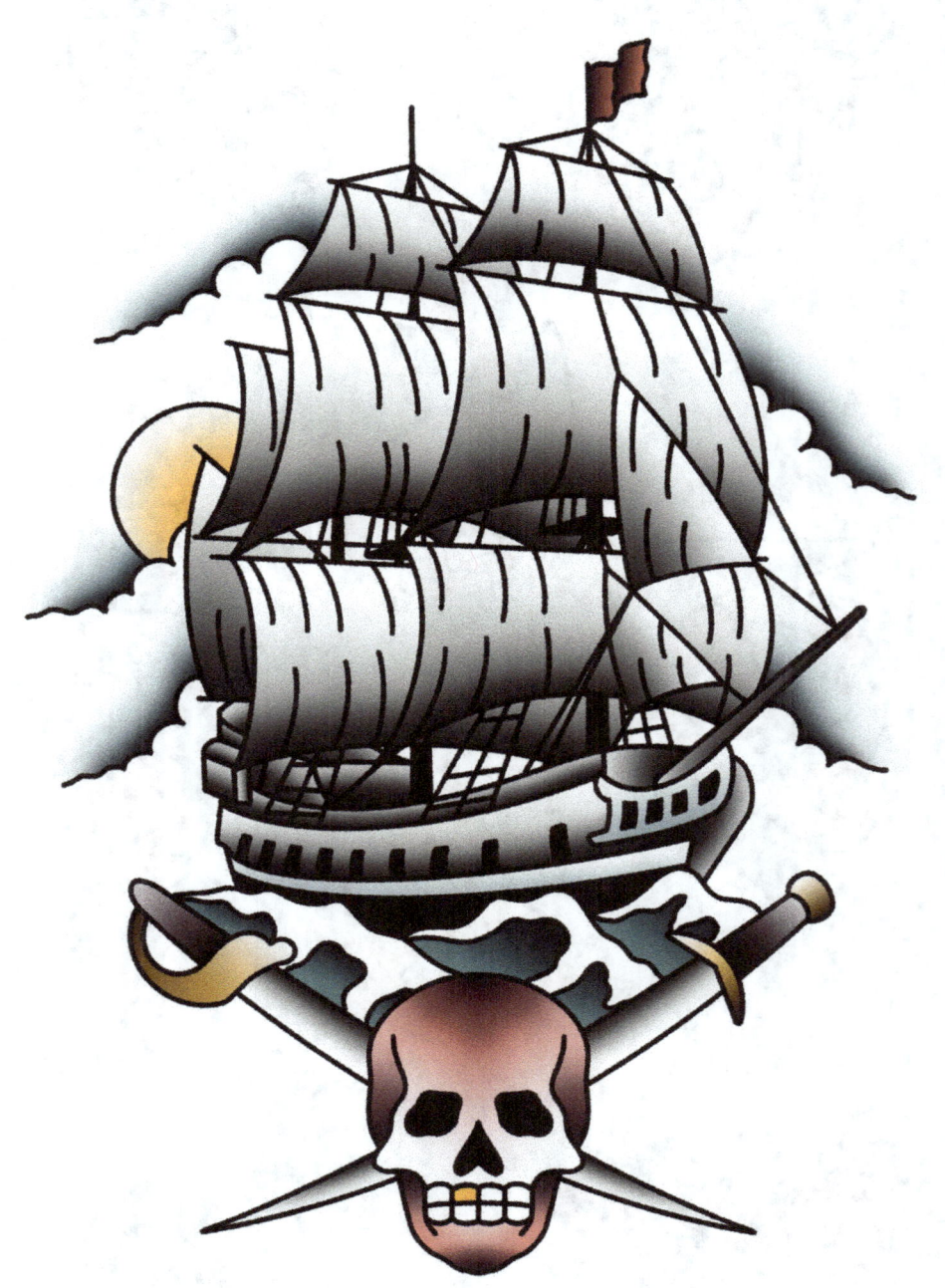

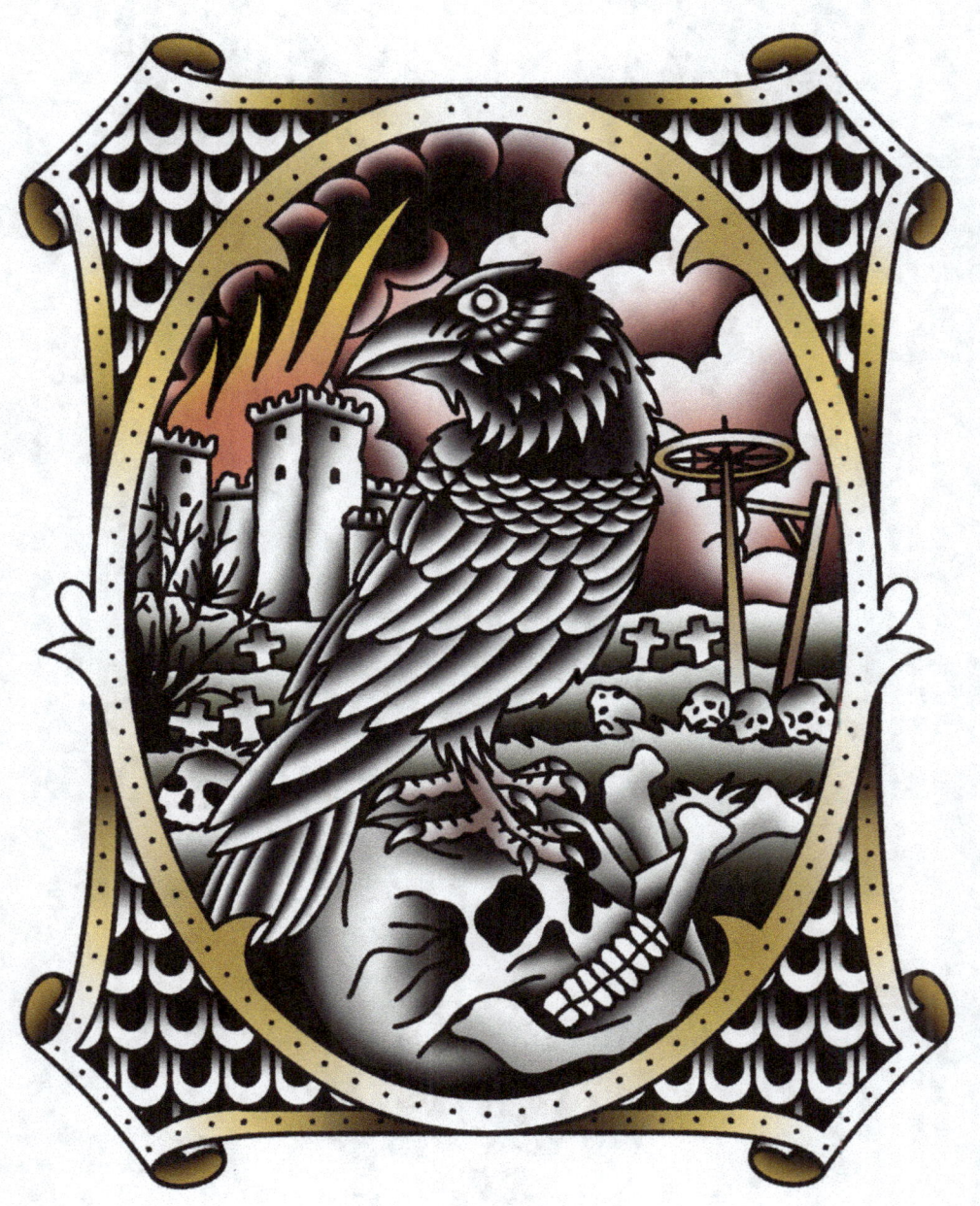

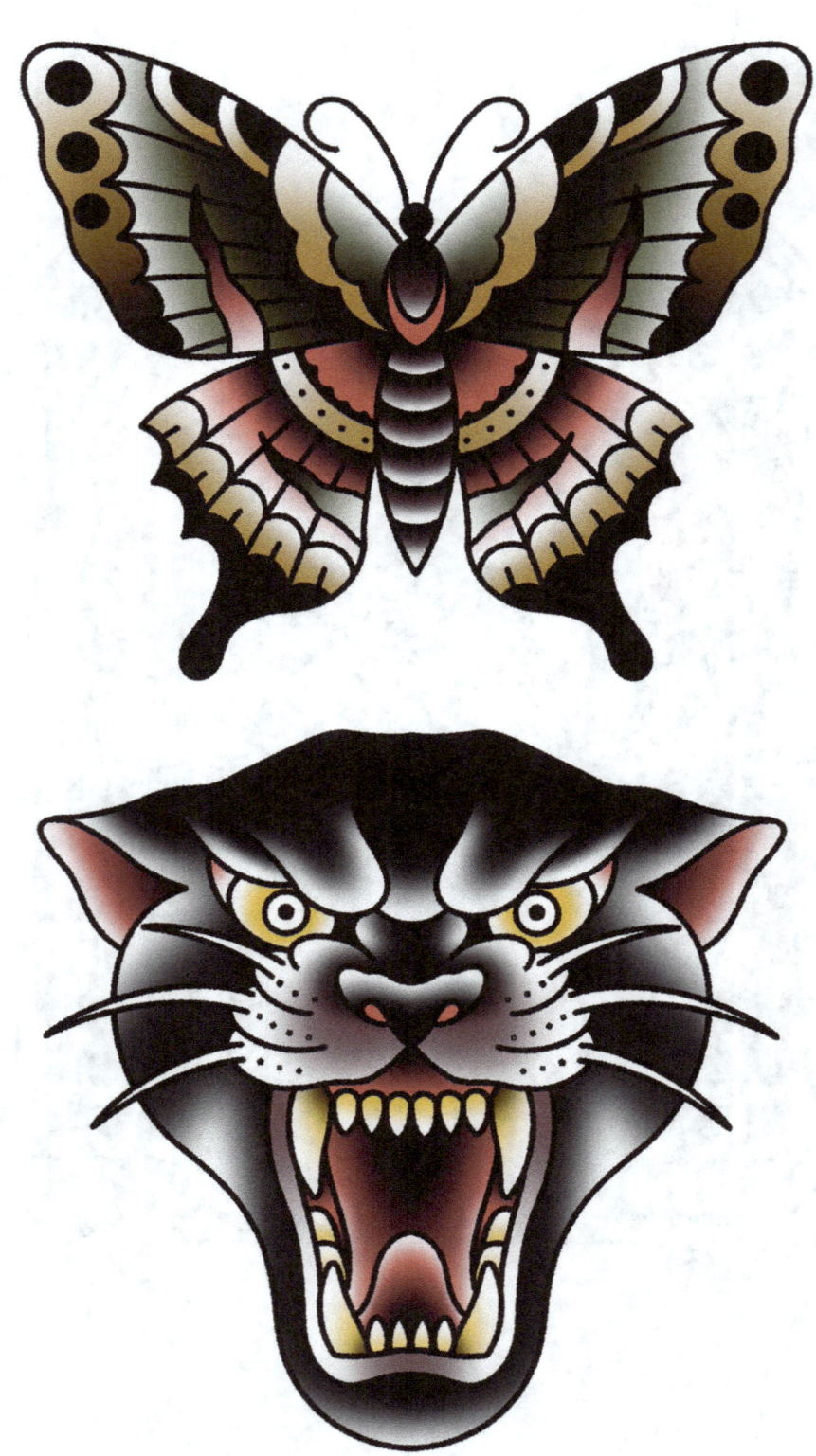

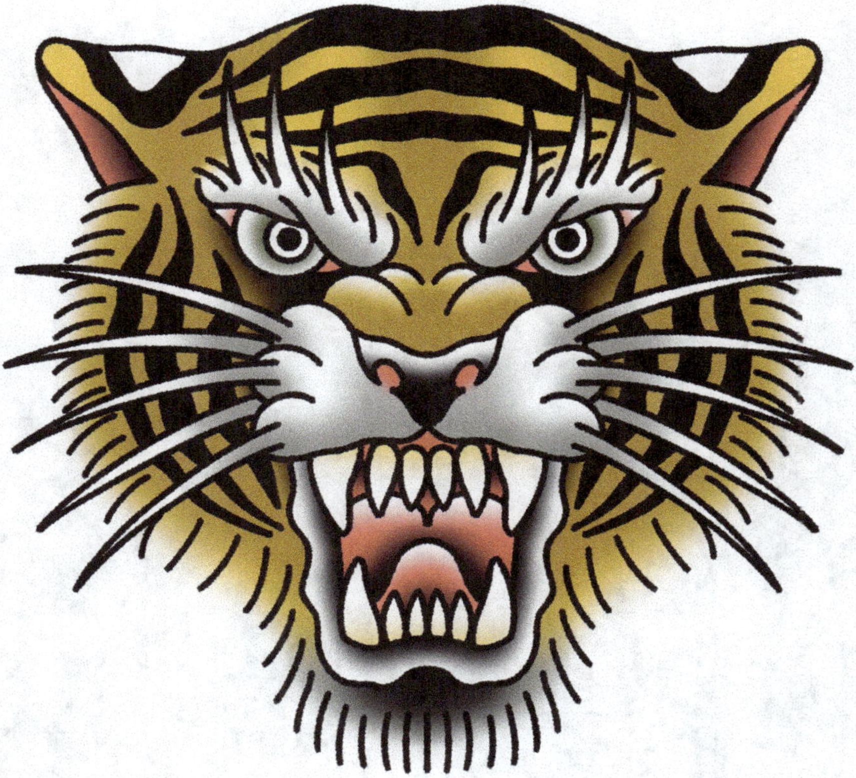

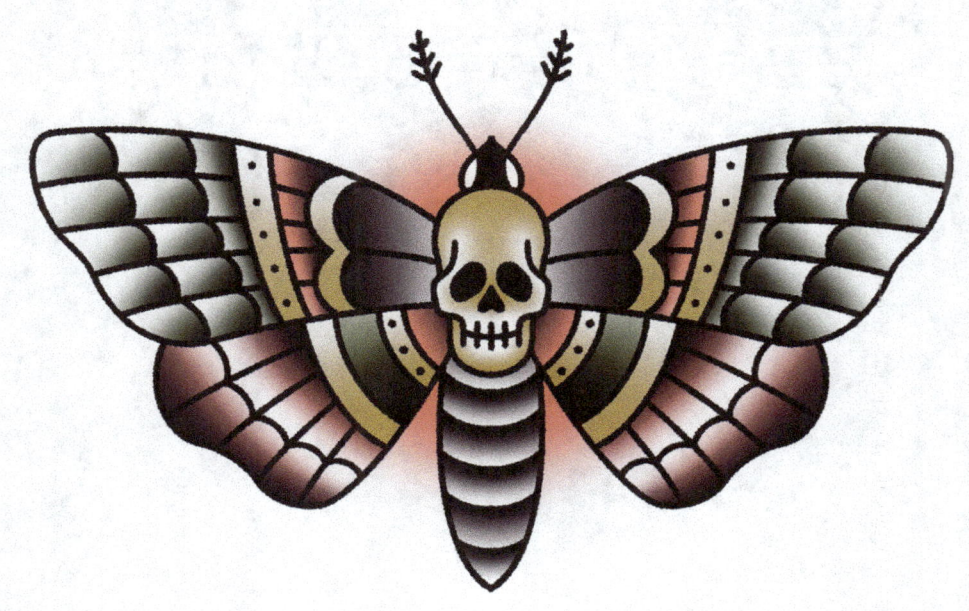

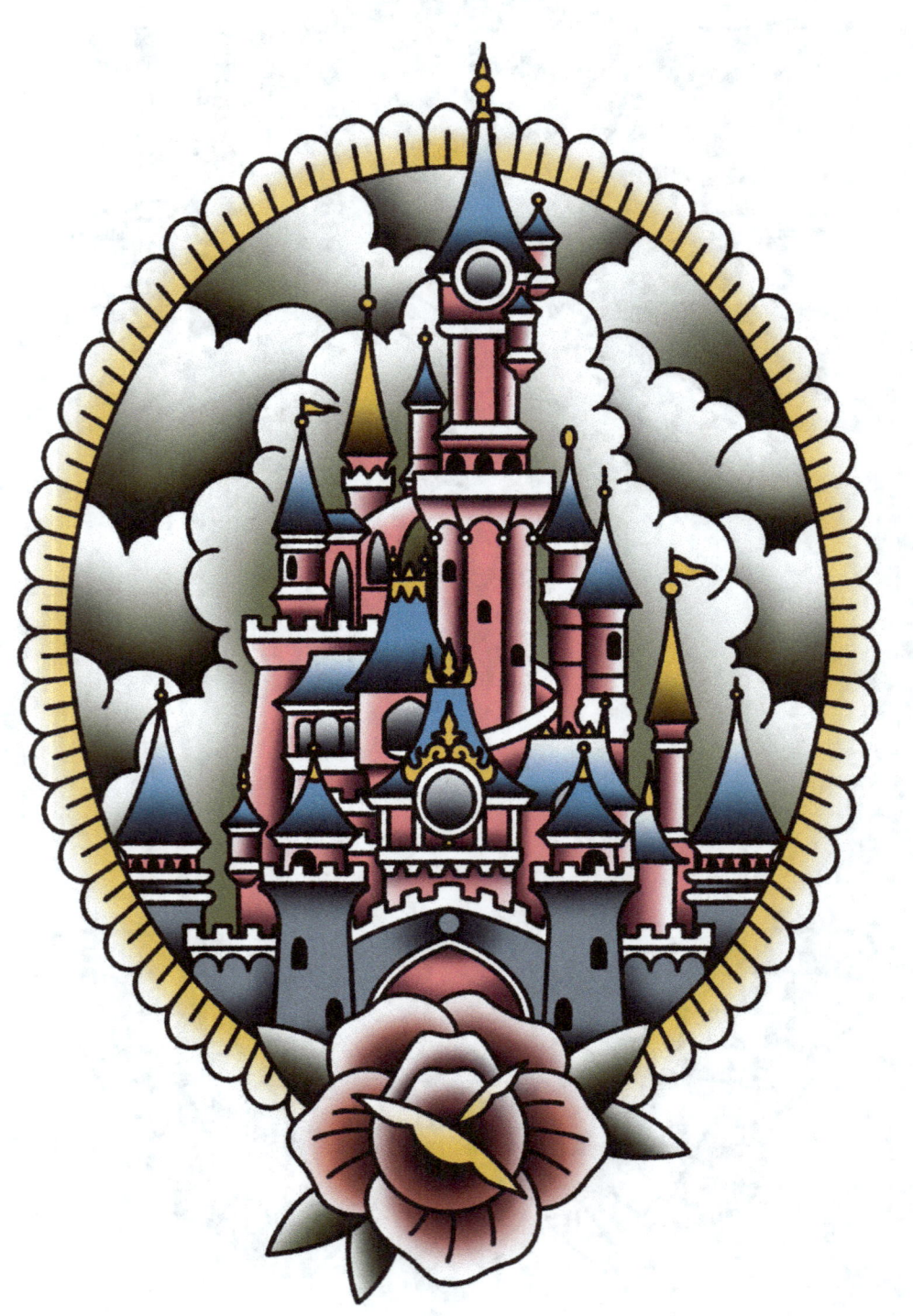

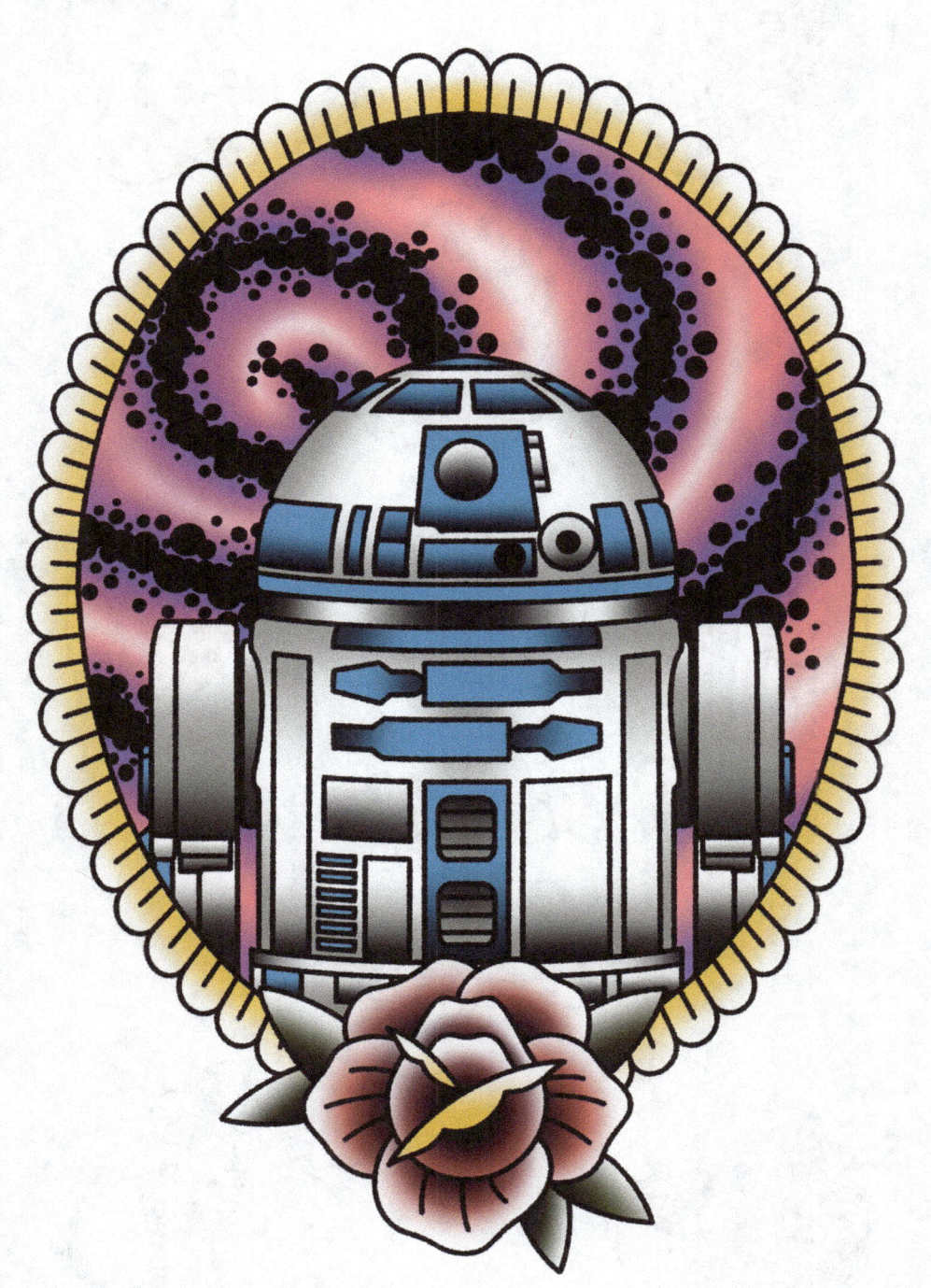

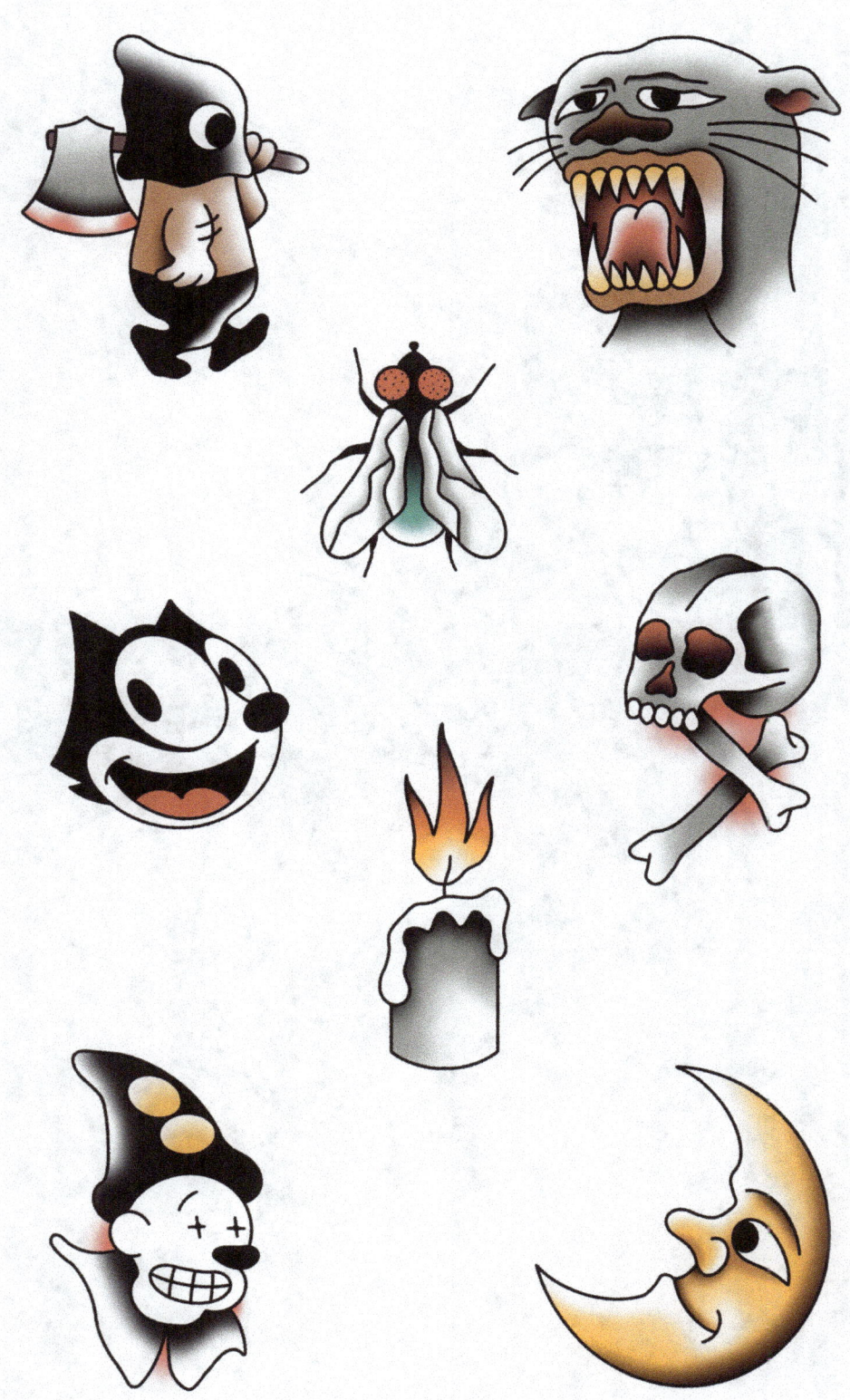

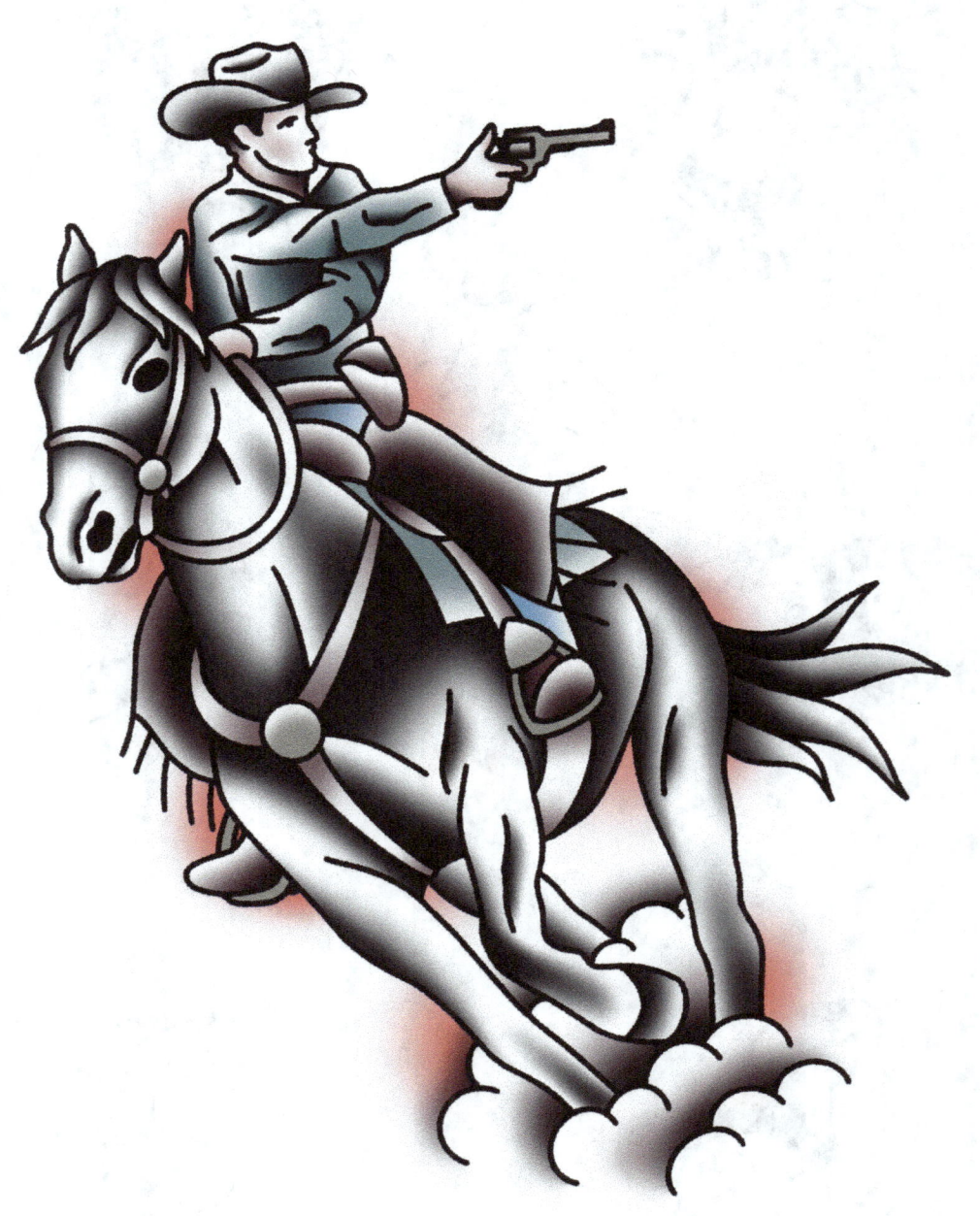

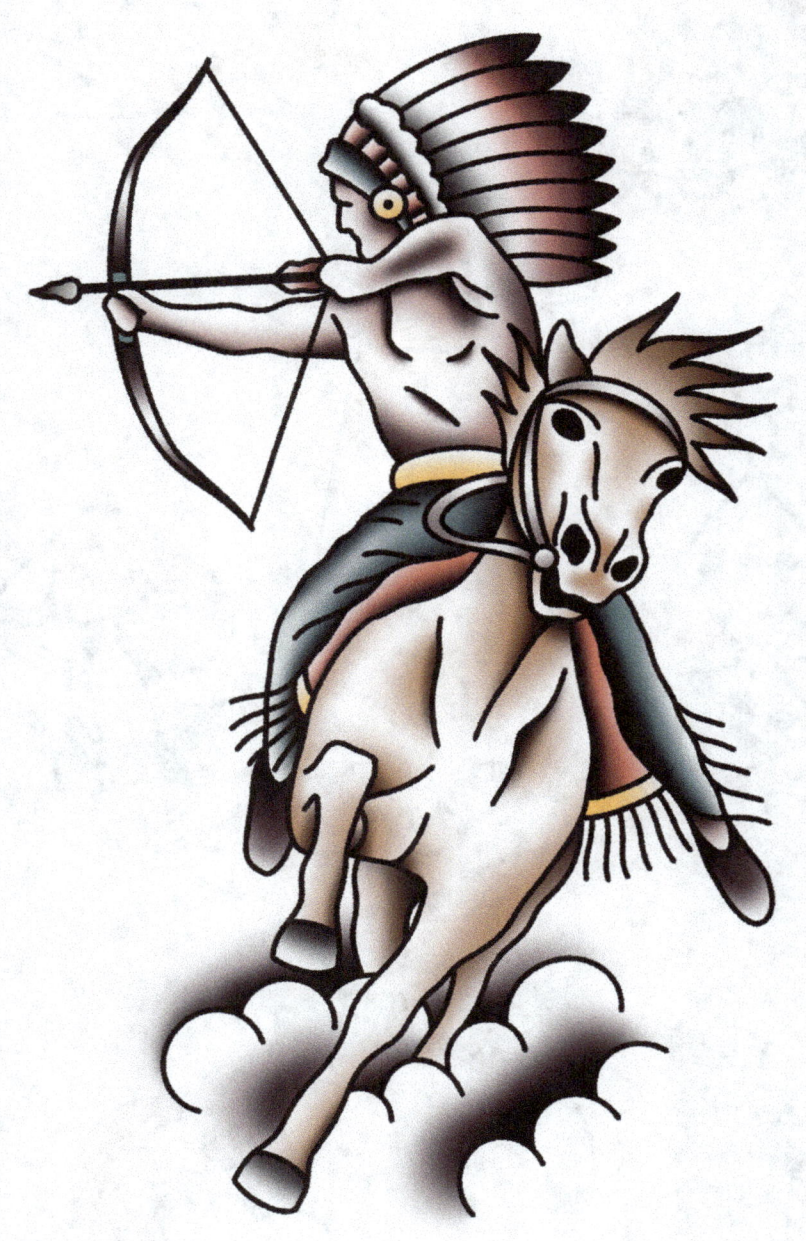

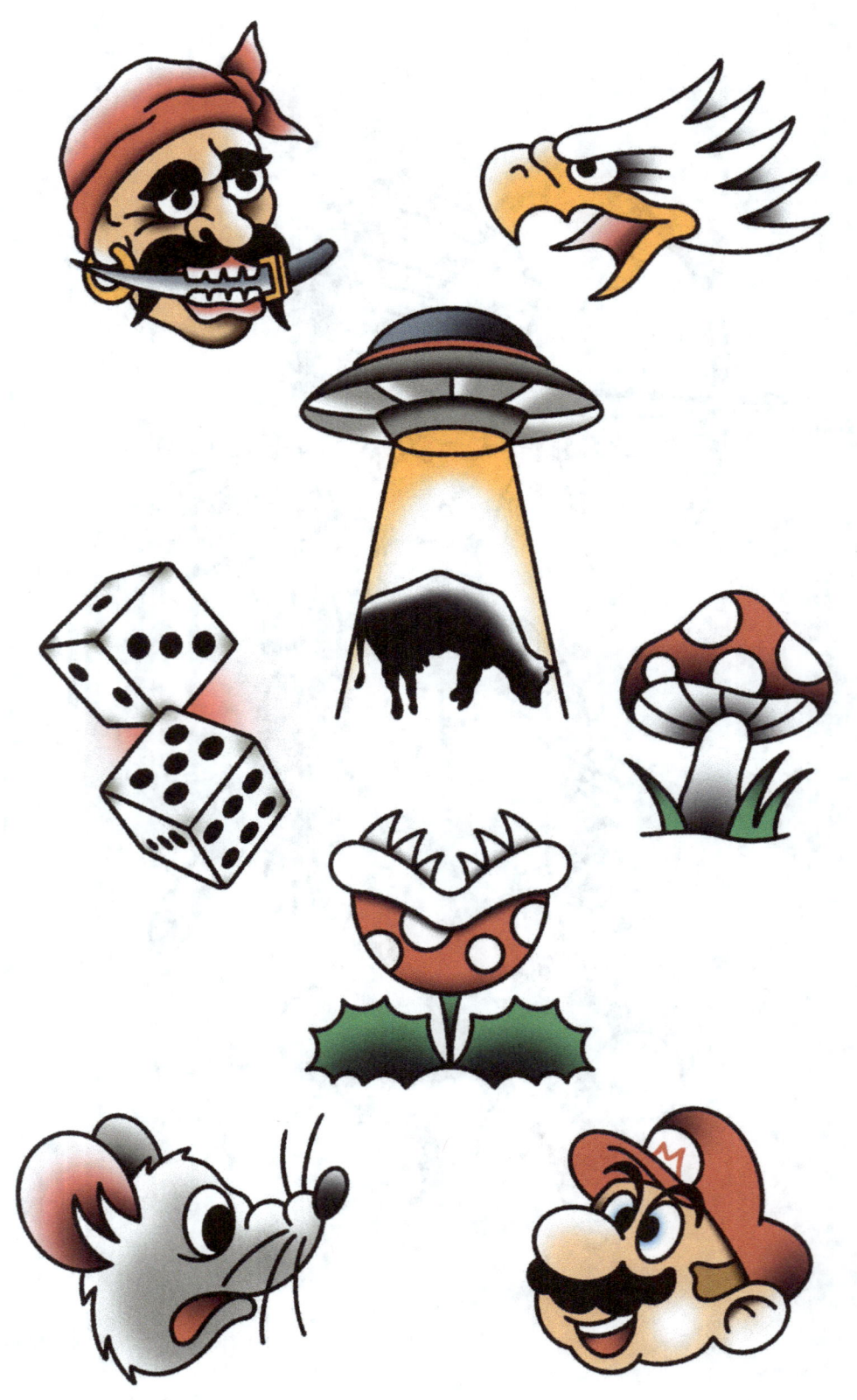

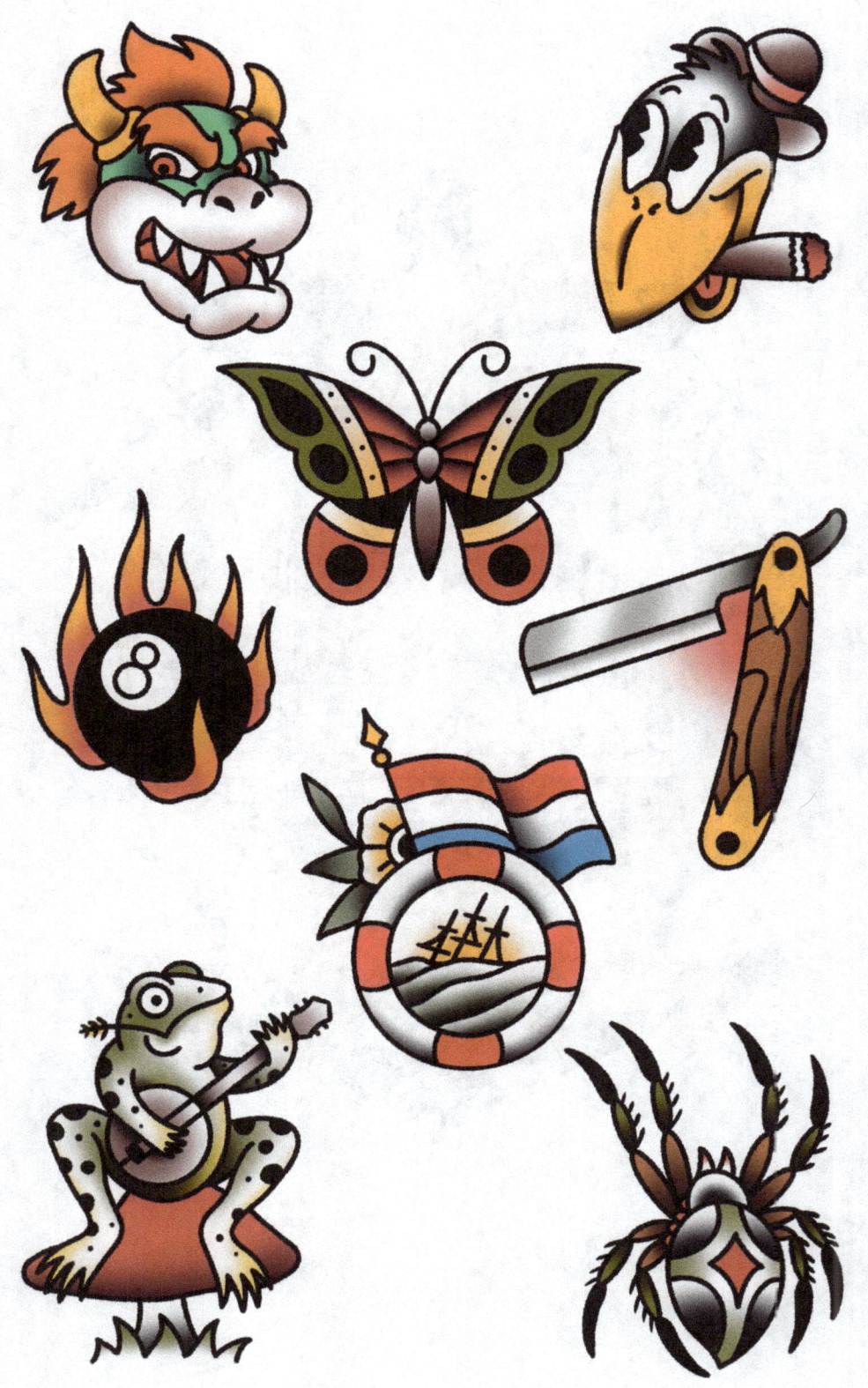

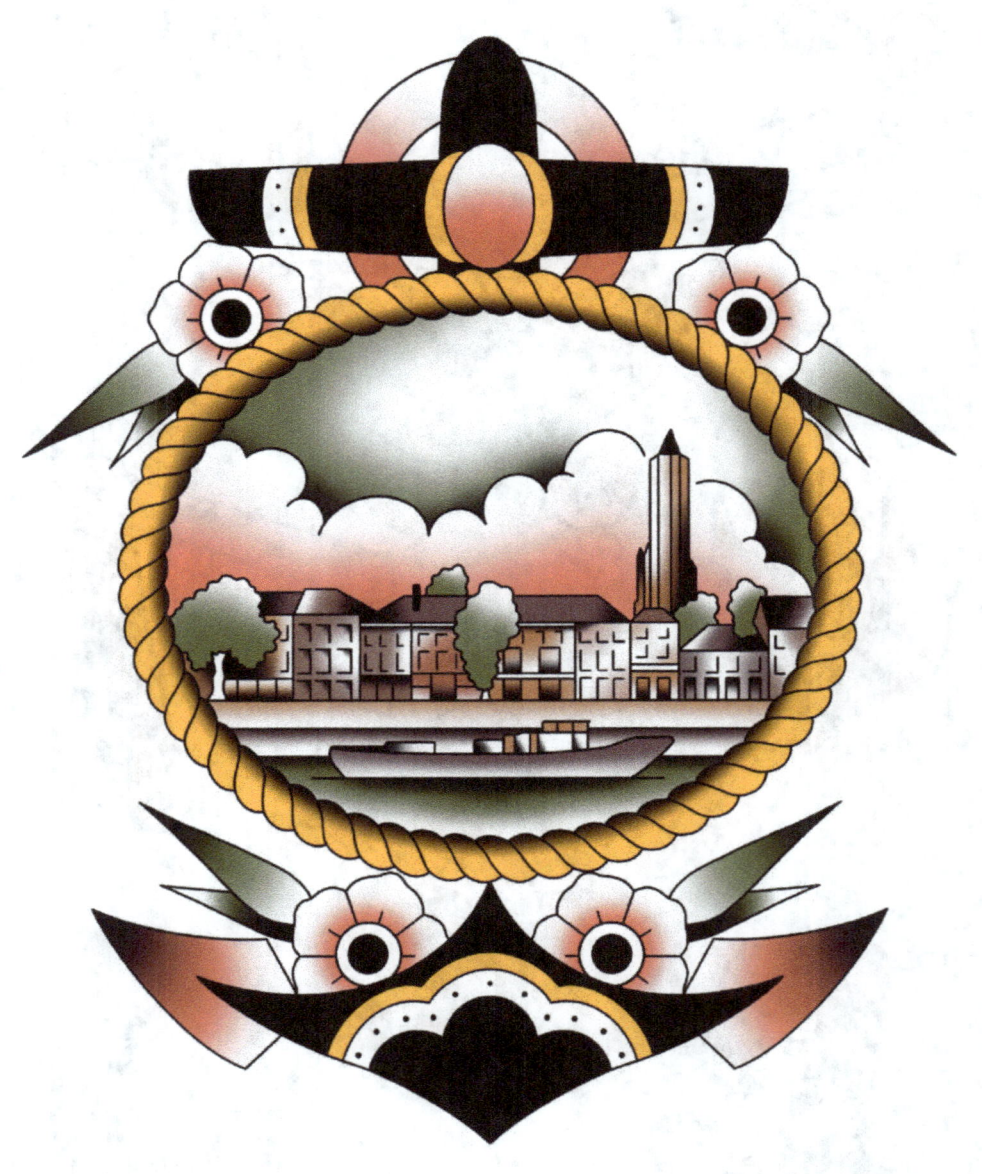

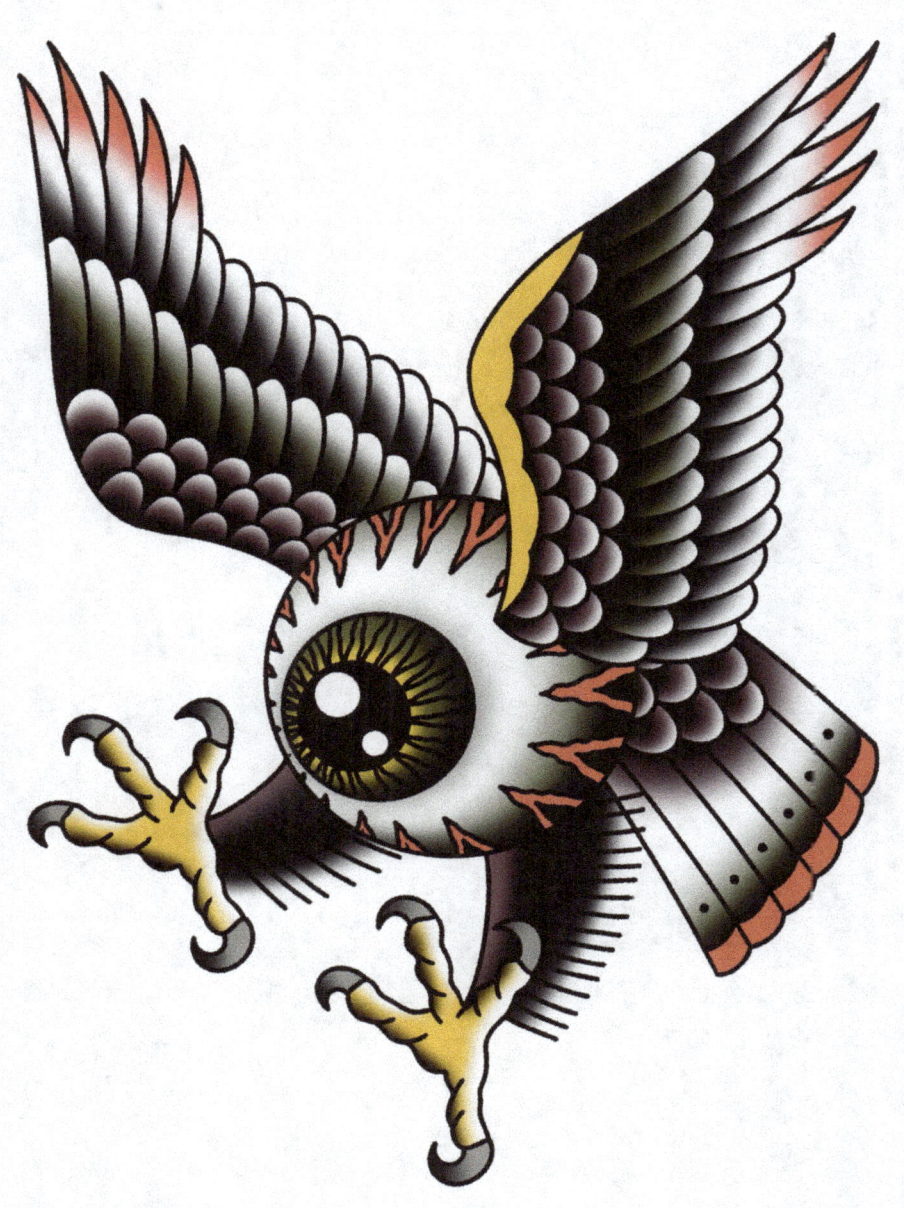

www.ingramcontent.com/pod-product-compliance
Lightning Source LLC
Chambersburg PA
CBHW071216240526
45470CB00018B/1888